Building Character in Schools Resource Guide

Karen E. Bohlin

Deborah Farmer

Kevin Ryan

JOSSEY-BASS
A Wiley Company
www.josseybass.com

Published by

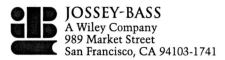

JOSSEY-BASS
A Wiley Company
989 Market Street
San Francisco, CA 94103-1741

www.josseybass.com

Jossey-Bass books and products are available through most bookstores. To contact Jossey-Bass directly, call (888) 378-2537, fax to (800) 605-2665, or visit our website at www.josseybass.com.

Substantial discounts on bulk quantities of Jossey-Bass books are available to corporations, professional associations, and other organizations. For details and discount information, contact the special sales department at Jossey-Bass.

We at Jossey-Bass strive to use the most environmentally sensitive paper stocks available to us. Our publications are printed on acid-free recycled stock whenever possible, and our paper always meets or exceeds minimum GPO and EPA requirements.

Library of Congress Cataloging-in-Publication Data

Bohlin, Karen E.
Building character in schools resource guide / Karen E. Bohlin, Deborah Farmer, Kevin Ryan.— 1st ed.
p. cm. — (The Jossey-Bass education series)
Companion vol. to: Building character in schools / Kevin Ryan, ©1999.
Includes bibliographical references (p.   ) and index.
ISBN 0-7879-5954-5 (alk. paper)
1. Moral education—United States. 2. Character—Study and teaching—United States.
I. Farmer, Deborah Lynn, 1955- II. Ryan, Kevin. III. Ryan, Kevin. Building character in schools.
IV. Title. V. Series.
LC311 .B57 2001
370.11'4—dc21   2001006046

FIRST EDITION
PB Printing   10 9 8 7 6 5 4 3 2 1

Contents

List of Exhibits, Checklists, and Worksheets

WORKSHEETS

Preface

IN THE WAKE of Columbine and Santee, perhaps there is no topic of greater importance than the development of good character in children and the example of character we offer them as educators and parents.

Growing rates of violence, victimization, and discontent in schools have driven some to give up hope of educating for character in schools today. A recent Josephson Institute of Ethics study found that one out of five high school boys carried a weapon to school. Seventy-five percent of boys and 60 percent of girls surveyed reported that in the past year they had hit someone out of anger.[1] Statistics on bullying are equally startling. A recent study by the National Institute of Child Health and Human Development of 15,686 public and private school students reported that bullying affects almost one of every three U.S. children in the sixth through the tenth grades.[2] Even more disturbing, according to a study by the Massachusetts Department of Health, in the past year alone 10 percent of the 4,000 Massachusetts high school student respondents reported that they had attempted to commit suicide.[3]

Psychologists continually remind us that young people as well as adults long for a moral center that enables them to make sense of their lives. If schools—alongside parents—do not offer children worthy goals and a vision for their lives, someone or something else will, without qualms about making power, deceit, casual sex, and consumerism attractive and worthy of pursuit.

In order to combat these competing visions of what is worthwhile, parents and educators must declare with conviction, "What I care about most is who you are and the kind of person you will become." Two dangers, however, threaten our perseverance in sustaining authentic character education: giving up and giving in.

We give up when we dwell on the disheartening statistics pointing to an increasing sense of anger, victimization, and alienation among students today and throw up our hands in despair. When we become disappointed, cynical, and even fearful for the safety and happiness of children, when we bemoan the situation, point the finger, and blame the schools, we offer very little support and guidance to young people looking to take their cue from us.

Equally as dangerous as giving up is giving in. A school outside Philadelphia seeks to stem problems by offering students who take *nonviolence pledges* limousine rides. Education officials in some states continue to discuss the possibility of mandating *courtesy clauses*, which would compel students to address their teachers as "Sir" or "Ma'am." Bullying prevention and social skills training programs have become a robust cottage industry. And schools across the nation continue to rely on organizations that peddle banners, bumper stickers, and student medals celebrating good character as incentives for being good.

We give in when we aim low. We settle for the quick fix, the purchased program, the set of narrowly prescribed behaviors, or the banner on the wall encouraging random acts of kindness. When we give in, we perpetuate a view of character education as medicine rather than as food, as programming students from without rather than strengthening them from within. We make it a remedy for problems instead of a means to health, maturity, friendship, and flourishing.

The preface to *Building Character in Schools* made reference to what Stephen Covey calls a paradigm shift away from a "personality ethic" toward a "character ethic."[4] Interest in character represents a desire for dispositions and qualities that are deeper and more stable than a positive attitude or an openness about feelings. The how-to-win-friends-and-influence-people mentality, with its focus on external behavior and social skills, has dominated our popular psychology and culture. It is still very much with us today, but there are signs of hope. We have been gradually turning our attention to something deeper and more fundamentally human: the centrality of character in a flourishing life.

This resource guide, a companion to *Building Character in Schools*, is designed to help educators in schools, homes, and communities set their sights higher, to ascribe to a goal worthy of our collective commitment. This goal is to help students flourish, to help them live virtuously in all spheres of life—personal, social, civic, and professional.

Building Character in Schools offers readers a theoretical and practical context for understanding and teaching character education in this increasingly pluralistic society. In that book, we provide readers with reasons, definitions, and arguments as well as illustrations and guidelines for developing virtue, the most stable building block of good character.

In the present book, *Building Character in Schools Resource Guide*, we provide the professional development blueprint for facilitating a school community's study, reflection, dialogue, and strategic planning. This guide allows educators to do their own in-depth teacher education and implementation of virtue-centered character education. Our centerpiece is a planning instrument titled Internalizing Virtue: An Instructional and Schoolwide Framework. This framework provides a set of lenses and questions that will help you develop an integrated approach to character education. The framework ensures that all of your efforts will raise students' awareness of virtue, inspire understanding, build good habits of action, and foster reflection. In short, application of the Internalizing Virtue Framework can help all the students and adults in your school to develop good habits of mind, heart, *and* action.

The BCIS Resource Guide is user friendly. In this book you will find key principles and central ideas, questions for reflection and discussion, worksheets, strategic planning checklists, and best practice stories from exemplary schools around the country. Each chapter presents focused activities, and the appendices offer a substantial collection of curriculum and classroom materials.

We have found that teachers and educational leaders long to be afforded the time for sustained study of and reflection on the purposes of education, the climate of their schools, the content of their curriculum, and the ideas and approaches that can make a lasting difference in the lives of their students. We know that you, the educators, are in the best position to lead this dialogue, exercise good judgment, make decisions, and effect change in your respective school communities.

In addition to time, teachers need guiding principles and tools to move character education from theory (and sound bites) to thoughtful practice. This guide invites you to sit down by yourself or with your colleagues and think about, plan, and operationalize an integrated approach to character education—one that suits your school community's distinctive needs.

Audience

We invite classroom teachers, administrators, task force leaders, and policymakers to use this guide as they lead in-service professional development seminars, grade-level team meetings, or department meetings. Because parents are the primary character educators of their children, we urge parent-teacher groups to use the guide in their collaboration with the school. We encourage educational leaders and consultants to use the material in this book in their presentations. However you choose to use this book, we would love to hear from you. We welcome your stories, comments, ideas, and suggestions. Please send them to us care of Jossey-Bass.

Overview of the Chapters

To assist educators who are using this resource guide and *Building Character in Schools* together, the chapters in this guide parallel the chapters in *BCIS*. We begin in Chapter One by defining character education and laying out the reasons why schools should undertake this challenge. Chapter Two first describes why an approach that teaches *virtue* is more helpful to children than approaches that teach *values* or *views*. It then takes you through a framework for helping children internalize virtue and the steps that build a firm foundation for character education in your school. The importance of turning the school into a community of virtue is discussed in Chapter Three, and methods of making character education an integral part of the curriculum are the focus of Chapter Four. Chapters Five, Six, and Seven discuss the specific roles and responsibilities of parents, teachers, and students, respectively.

Overview of the Appendices

The two appendices in Part One, "Good Ideas," offer readings with both practical and philosophical support for character education. Teachers working in groups will find materials for thought-provoking discussion here. The appendices in Part Two, "Action Strategies," present a variety of practical tools to help you design character education activities, set standards for children of different ages, and begin the practice of teaching children to reflect on their behavior. Part Three, "Curriculum," contains sample units that illustrate many ways of incorporating the teaching of virtue into the curriculum. All the appendices may be adapted for your own use; forms and surveys are designed to be reproducible.

The best practice stories that follow most major sections in each chapter also offer many examples of effective character education ideas and strategies from schools around the country.

How to Use This Resource Guide

We hope this guide helps you and your colleagues to develop more confidence, competence, and conviction in educating for academic and character excellence. You may use it one chapter at a time or as a whole during a series of meetings throughout the year. You may also find it useful as a guide for planning during a task force or faculty retreat.

We particularly encourage you to complete the discussion and reflection activities in the chapters. They are an integral part of this book, helping you to develop a firm philosophical foundation for building character in your students and to formulate ideas and approaches especially appropriate for your school. Ideally, they will be completed by a group of educators working together and sharing thoughts and experiences. Moreover, these activities are designed to be cumulative; they will be most useful and productive when you and your colleagues can engage in them in the order in which they appear.

Acknowledgments

Whenever we set about to write for educators, we are reminded of those teachers, parents, students, school leaders, colleagues, and friends who educate the minds and characters of young people on a daily basis. This resource guide is inspired by their dedication and example.

We would also like to acknowledge those who have helped to make this book possible. First, we thank Lesley Iura and Christie Hakim at Jossey-Bass for inviting us to write this companion to *Building Character in Schools*. We are also grateful to Virginia Roberts Holt and Mary Anne Presberg of the Full Circle Family Foundation, who generously supported this project.

We are grateful to the Character Education Partnership (CEP) and the National Schools of Character (NSOC) Awards Program. Several of the best practice stories in this guide come from schools that received awards in 1998, 1999, and 2000. We enjoyed the great privilege of working closely with CEP on this project and visiting many of these exemplary schools.[5]

We owe special thanks to Michael Lynberg for his editorial assistance and to our colleagues and staff at the Center for the Advancement of Ethics and Character at Boston University, who were enormously helpful as we brought this resource book to completion, especially Megan Black and Erika Bachiochi. We are indebted to Steven Tigner for his generous contributions to this guide and to all of you who permitted us to share your outstanding work with our readers. We thank all the participants and presenters in our professional development institutes and Teachers Academies, who have not only piloted many of the activities in this book but have also inspired their development and revision. We are particularly grateful to the schools in Bourne, Lynn, Brighton, and Ware, Massachusetts, and to the teachers and administrators we have worked with in Georgia, New Hampshire, and South Carolina. Finally, we are grateful to Alison Reichert and Kathleen Clifford of the Boston

University School of Education for their unwavering technical assistance and support.

October 2001   KAREN E. BOHLIN
Boston   DEBORAH FARMER
                                                                   KEVIN RYAN

Chapter 1

Character Education

What Is It and Why Is It Important?

> Sow a thought and reap an act;
> Sow an act and you reap a habit;
> Sow a habit and you reap a character;
> Sow a character and you reap a destiny.
>
> —ANONYMOUS

> You don't get to choose how you're going to die. Or when.
> You can only decide how you're going to live.
>
> —JOAN BAEZ

TODAY, VOICES from within and beyond our schools are calling for a return to a focus on *character education*—a focus that has been missing from many schools since the late 1960s. This widely popular movement is gathering support from people across the political spectrum and from all facets of society. Character education, however, is not simply a movement or an educational fad; it is central to good teaching and learning. It is, in fact, the schools' oldest mission and crucial to both moral *and* intellectual development.

The Development of Good Character

What does it mean to talk about *character* and *character education*? The English word *character* comes from the Greek word *charassein*, which means "to engrave," as on a wax tablet, a gemstone, or a metal surface. From that root evolved the meaning of character as a distinctive mark or sign, and from that meaning grew our conception of character as, in the words of *Webster's New World Dictionary of the American Language*, "an individual's pattern of behavior . . . his moral constitution."

The development of good character is about fostering the *habits of mind, heart, and action* that enable an individual to flourish, that is, to use his or her time, talent, and energy well, to become the best he or she can be. Habits of mind, heart, and action are intimately connected.

- *Good habits of mind* include developing the ability to sum up a situation, deliberate, choose the right thing to do, and then do it. Aristotle called this *practical wisdom*. It is about choosing well in all spheres of life.

- *Good habits of the heart* include developing a full range of moral feelings and emotions, including love for good and contempt for evil, as well as the capacity to empathize with others. These habits are about wanting to do what is right.

- *Good habits of action* include having the *will* to act once we have thoughtfully considered all the circumstances and relevant facts. The world is filled with people who know what the right thing to do is but who lack the corresponding habit of action, the will to carry it out.

When we have good character, more is demanded from us than merely an intellectual commitment, a heartfelt desire, or a mechanical fulfillment of responsibilities. We are motivated to do the right thing and to avoid the wrong—even if that wrong will never be found out, even when we are under pressure (for example, the pressure to cheat to keep a certain grade point average).

▶ Key Thoughts

Education in its fullest sense is inescapably a moral enterprise—a continuous and conscious effort to guide students to know and pursue what is good and what is worthwhile. Therefore character education is not about simply acquiring a set of behaviors. It is about developing the habits of mind, heart, and action that enable a person to flourish.

▶ Discussion and Reflection Activities

To delve further into the components of good character, consider these questions:

- If you were to describe someone as having good character, what would you mean by that statement?

- If you could invite a historical figure to be your school's adviser-in-residence, who would this person be? What would you want your students to learn from his or her teachings and example?

Character Education Is Respectful of Different Cultures, Religions, and Creeds

Character education is about teaching our students how to make wise decisions and act on them. It is about helping them live a good life and contribute to the good of society. But what does it mean to live a *good life,* and what is *the good*? People differ somewhat in how they define it, but there is a huge overlap of common understandings across religious traditions, cultures, and time. Some form of the Golden Rule, for example, exists in almost every culture (see Exhibit 1.1).

Additionally, in the world's literature, religions, philosophies, and art we find a huge deposit of shared moral values. The ideals that the ancient Greeks called the cardinal virtues show up most frequently, cutting across history and cultures. The Greeks named these ideals wisdom (also called good judgment or prudence), justice, self-mastery (or temperance), and courage (or fortitude). *Wisdom* is the virtue that enables us to exercise sound

---

EXHIBIT 1.1

The Golden Rule

If we live according to the guidance of reason, we shall desire for others the good which we seek for ourselves.

—Baruch Spinoza

Help thy brother's boat across and lo! thine own has reached the shore.

—Hindu proverb

Judaism: *What is hateful to you, do not to your fellow man. That is the entire law; all the rest is commentary.*

—The Talmud, Shabbat 31

Christianity: *Do to others as you would have them do to you.*

—Luke 6:31

Islam: *None of you has faith unless he loves for his brother what he loves for himself.*

—Hadith (Bukhari) 2:6

Buddhism: *Hurt not others in ways that you yourself would find hurtful.*

—Udana Varga

Hinduism: *This is the sum of duty: Do naught unto others which would cause you pain if done to you.*

—The Mahabharata

Confucianism: *"Is there one word that will keep us on the path to the end of our days?"*
"Yes, Reciprocity. What you do not wish yourself, do not unto others."

—The Analects

judgment in planning and taking the right course of action in our pursuit of what is right and good. *Justice* is an other-regarding, or social, virtue, concerned with our personal, professional, and legal obligations and commitments to others. *Self-mastery,* in contrast, is an inner virtue that gives us intelligent control over our impulses and fosters moral autonomy. Lastly, *courage,* knowing what is to be feared and what is not to be feared, is the steadfastness to commit ourselves to what is good and right and actively pursue it, even when it is not convenient or popular. These virtues are called *cardinal,* from the Latin *cardo,* or "hinge," "that on which something turns or depends," because most other virtues are related to one or more of them. Exhibit 1.2 presents a number of these related virtues.

EXHIBIT 1.2

Cardinal Virtues and Related Virtues

1. Courage (or Fortitude)
   Related virtues
   Loyalty
   Hope
   Perseverance
   Generosity (giving without expecting anything in return)
2. Self-Mastery (or Temperance)
   Related virtues
   Patience
   Diligence
   Gratitude
   Courtesy
   Order
3. Justice
   Related virtues
   Responsibility
   Citizenship
   Dependability or reliability
   Respect
   Sportsmanship
   Kindness/compassion
4. Wisdom (or Good Judgment or Prudence)
   Related virtues
   Honesty
   Integrity
   Humility

According to Aristotle, a virtue is a disposition to choose well.[1] A virtue usually lies on a mean between two vices—one of excess and one of deficiency. For example, courage, which means knowing what is to be feared and not to be feared, lies between excessive fear or cowardice on the one hand and a deficiency of fear or recklessness on the other (see Exhibit 1.3). We can place a virtue such as kindness on this Aristotelian scale too. If we define kindness as the disposition to show care and concern for others, an excess of care for another person could manifest itself as the vice of saccharine sweetness or obsequiousness whereas a deficiency in caring could appear as mean-spiritedness.

Certain virtues are universal. They are the intellectual and moral habits that are vital not only to our personal well-being but to the well-being of the society in which we live.

▶ Key Thoughts

Character education is respectful of our multiethnic, multireligious, and multicultural society and seeks to impart certain universally recognized dispositions and habits that are vital to our personal and collective well-being.

▶ Discussion and Reflection Activities

Use these activities as a means of reflecting on virtues that everyone believes are important:

- Think of a person you admire whose background is dissimilar from your own. What intellectual and moral qualities did or does this person possess?

EXHIBIT 1.3

The Aristotelian Scale

Action or Feeling	Excess	Mean	Deficiency
Fear and confidence	Recklessness	Courage	Cowardice
Pleasure and pain	Self-indulgence	Self-mastery	Self-neglect
Giving	Wastefulness	Generosity	Stinginess
Anger	Irascibility	Patience	Lack of spirit
Self-expression	Boastfulness	Truthfulness	Mock-modesty
Social conduct	Obsequiousness	Friendliness	Cantankerousness
Hope	Presumption/Naive happy-think	Optimism	Pessimism
Shame	Shyness	Modesty	Shamelessness

Source: Adapted from Aristotle, *Ethics,* J.A.K. Thomson, trans. (London: Penguin Books, 1976).

- Review the list of cardinal virtues and related virtues in Exhibit 1.2. Explain how the related virtues depend on the cardinal virtue in each case. What related virtues would you add to this list?

- Looking back at Exhibit 1.3, identify other virtues that lie on a mean between two extremes: a vice of excess and a vice of deficiency. For example, kindness, as mentioned, may be said to lie between saccharine sweetness and mean-spiritedness; diligence may be said to lie between workaholism and laziness.

The Arguments for Character Education

You are probably aware that some teachers, administrators, and others are quite ambivalent about involving schools in character education. In fact, many people are vehemently opposed to it. Thus, if you believe that character education is important, it helps to know the main arguments in favor of it. There are five of them:

Argument 1: Inevitability

Children cannot enter the educational system at age four and stay until age seventeen without having their character and moral values profoundly affected by the experience, for better or for worse. Further, becoming a serious student is one of the great ethical challenges the majority of our children face during their youth. In short, character education is inevitable, so we should be intentional about helping children to develop good habits (or virtues) and to struggle against bad ones.

Argument 2: Our Nation's Founders

The second argument in favor of character education is that of our nation's founders. The founders' writings, particularly those of Thomas Jefferson, James Madison, John Adams, Abigail Adams, and Benjamin Franklin, are filled with admonitions that the new republic must make character education a high priority. To work as it should, democracy demands an educated and virtuous citizenry.

Argument 3: State Laws

The third argument is found in our state codes of education, which direct the operations of our schools. These state codes overwhelmingly support actively teaching the core moral values that provide the social glue of civic life. Currently, all fifty states address character education either directly or indirectly. By *indirectly* we mean that they establish outcomes and standards that focus on the responsibilities of democratic citizenship or on particular attributes of civility. No state codes of education or state standards outlaw, forbid, or in any way discourage character education.

Argument 4: The Will of the People

The fourth argument comes from the citizens of this country. For many years, the Gallup Organization and other polling companies have been asking the American people about their views on the performance of public schools and related topics. Ninety percent or more of adults support the teaching of honesty (97 percent), democracy (93 percent), acceptance of people of different races and ethnic backgrounds (91 percent), patriotism (91 percent), caring for friends and family members (91 percent), moral courage (91 percent), and the Golden Rule (90 percent) in the public schools.[2]

Argument 5: Intellectual Authorities

The world's great thinkers from the West, including Plato, Aristotle, Kant, and Dewey, and from the East, including Confucius, Lao-tzu, and Buddha, have all been strong advocates of giving our conscious attention to character formation and focusing our energies on living worthy lives. In recent decades, however, in the midst of what has been called a knowledge explosion, and faced with increasing questions about what in this noisy modern world is good and worthwhile, many educators have turned their attention to the development of processes and skills—reading, writing, and data storage and retrieval. Although these skills are important, they leave to others the teaching of our culture's core ethical values.

The Lesson of Experience

In addition to these arguments, we should recall the lesson of experience. In the 1950s, many people had the sense that individuals in this country held a set of shared ideals and attitudes about respect and responsibility, hard work, and citizenship. Such virtues were taught directly in the school.

In the sixties, with the opposition to the Vietnam War, the sexual revolution, and additional social tumult, moral authority was called into question. Teachers distanced themselves from students' moral development and attempted to become neutral facilitators, leaving students free to figure out life's toughest questions on their own and to view society's traditions of civility with skepticism and scorn. They were left free to arrive at their own values. This had deeply troubling results—relationships and respect eroded between adults and children, cynicism toward authority grew, and students were left morally adrift.

Some people argue that comparisons such as this, which hearken back to the days of *Leave It to Beaver*, are pure nostalgia for a Golden Age that never existed. They make the case that before the changes of the 1960s, students were narrowly indoctrinated, blindly obedient, and unreflective about their behavior and that important issues, such as racial injustice and women's rights, were largely ignored. Yet recognizing such deficiencies does not mean that character education automatically results in these problems, only that we can do better.

With our experience and the advantages of hindsight, we are now better positioned to help students internalize good habits of mind, heart, and action. As educators, we know the importance of providing them with the example, guidance, and coaching they need to use their freedom well.

▶ Key Thoughts

The world's great thinkers, our country's founders, the laws of the land, and popular sentiment all recognize character education as essential. However, in part because of the knowledge explosion and in part because they have not wanted to impose moral values on their students, many schools in recent decades have decided to focus on information processing skills and to leave character education to someone else.

▶ Discussion and Reflection Activities

To increase your ability to articulate the strong arguments for character education, reflect on these questions:

- Which argument for character education do you find most compelling and why?
- What arguments can you add to this list?
- How would you define and describe character education to parents in your school? How would you describe the purpose of character education to your students?

▶ Best Practice Story

Fifty-eight words. How do you sum up the mission, vision, and ethos of a school in fifty-eight words? Try this:

> *At Slavens we take the high road. We genuinely care about ourselves, each other and our school. We show and receive respect by using kind words and actions, listening thoughtfully, standing up for ourselves and others, and taking responsibility for our own behavior and learning. This is who we are even when no one is watching!*

This is the code of conduct at Slavens School, a K-8 school in Denver, Colorado, and it is not a dusty document. The Slavens community consistently uses these fifty-eight words to examine their thoughts, their actions, and their efforts to become an exemplary school.

The school created the code because, while teachers had individual classroom expectations, what they really longed for was a common set of goals and expectations that would resonate in the hallways, lunchroom, and playground. After creating a code of conduct, the faculty then had the task of not only presenting it to students, but helping it come alive in the life of the school and its pupils. This did not happen overnight. The school broke down the code sentence by sentence and put the sentences on pieces of paper throughout the school. They then asked students to take the part of the code they understood the least and write about it in terms of their personal experience: What does this mean to you? Teachers spent time in class reviewing various aspects of the code and looking for examples of these principles in history and literature. The drama teacher had students do skits in which they explored the aspects of the code. Through these efforts they started learning from each other's insights and their own understanding became more sophisticated. In an era of high profile, senseless and brutal acts by young people, take by contrast these two comments from Slavens students, "We think about our behavior. We think about what we are going to do before we do it," and "Taking the high road means we do what we know is right deep down. We [know] who we are in our hearts."

Chapter 2
Views, Values, or Virtues?

Great necessities call out great virtues.
—ABIGAIL ADAMS, letter to John Quincy Adams

All virtue is summed up in dealing justly.
—ARISTOTLE, *The Nicomachean Ethics*

It is not the brains that matter most, but that which guides
them—the character, the heart, generous qualities, progressive
ideas.
—FYODOR DOSTOEVSKY, *The Insulted and the Injured*

HOW CAN WE HELP students develop the strength of character they need to lead their lives well? This chapter analyzes popular approaches to character education, presents a framework you can use as a guide in helping students internalize virtue, and outlines the principles to follow and steps to take in establishing a community of virtue.

Distinguishing Views, Values, and Virtues

Some people argue that the *views* we have on an array of different issues provide our moral starting point. Others contend that our *values* constitute our moral compass. However, this book is premised on the belief that *virtues* are what orient us appropriately and strengthen our character. Virtues are the *keystone* of character education.

The Views Approach
Views are the intellectual positions we hold on a range of issues, from politics and the economy to religious practice, and the views-driven classroom

regularly engages students in discussions of controversial issues. In classrooms where views are emphasized, teachers believe that they are helping students develop a moral compass by helping them acquire strong views on social issues such as the environment, gun control, homosexual marriage, and prayer in school. This approach to moral issues is something like what you might see if you watch Oprah Winfrey or Jerry Springer. It might make for stimulating television, but it has little to do with character development. In general this approach generates more heat than light, and students are left with the impression that some issues are "just too complicated" or "ultimately just a matter of opinion."

The Values Approach

Values are what an individual wants, desires, or ascribes worth to. Some values are no more than matters of preference, like a taste for designer clothing. Some values are related to ethnic background and traditions, such as a French citizen's concern for his language. Some stem from religious beliefs, such as our attitudes toward the Sabbath. The things we value can be morally good, bad, or neutral. Moreover, values do not necessarily command our behavior: that is, we can value one thing and do another. In the current cultural climate, values are not only a matter of personal choice but also a personal right, not to be limited by one or another form of moral authority. Therefore one of the premises of the values-driven approach to character education, which is popular in many schools, is that teachers and schools should not indoctrinate or impose their values on students. Instead, schools should give students practice at sorting out their own values. There are no absolute moral standards or norms in this approach, only individual values.

The Virtues Approach

Virtues are habits cultivated within the individual that actually improve character and intelligence. The ancient Greek term for this concept was *arete ethike*, signifying "moral virtue," or "character excellence." The Greek word *arete* means "excellence." The equivalent Latin term was *virtus moralis.* As the novelist Pearl Buck wrote, "The secret of joy in work is contained in one word—excellence. To know how to do something well is to enjoy it."[1] Virtues—habits such as diligence, sincerity, personal accountability, courage, and perseverance—actually enable us to develop better relationships and to do our work better and thereby attain human excellence. It is our virtues, not our views or our values, that enable us to become better students, parents, spouses, teachers, friends, and citizens.

Whereas views are simply intellectual positions and values evoke neither a moral commitment nor the promise of leading a good life, virtues enable us to shape and lead worthy lives. Education in virtues—those good dispositions of the heart and mind that are regularly put into action—is the foundation of solid character development.

▶ Key Thoughts

The idea expressed here is summed up in *The Character Education Manifesto* (Appendix A) this way: "Character education is about developing virtues—good habits and dispositions which lead students to responsible and mature adulthood. Virtue ought to be our foremost concern in educating for character. Character education is not about acquiring the right views—currently accepted attitudes about ecology, prayer in school, gender, school uniforms, politics, or ideologically charged issues."

▶ Discussion and Reflection Activities

To begin identifying the core virtues that should be taught at your school, review the list of cardinal virtues and related virtues in Exhibit 1.2, and then answer these questions:

- Which of these virtues do you think your school is currently teaching?

- Which virtues would you like to emphasize more deliberately school-wide?

- Which of these virtues work in concert with the academic goals of your school?

- Which of these virtues support music, physical education, social interaction, and extracurricular activities?

Helping Students Internalize Virtue

Imagine the following scenario: you are a teacher, and one morning you get stuck in a traffic jam and arrive at school fifteen minutes late. You walk down the hall, imagining chaos. But as you approach your room, the emanating silence is almost more unnerving. Have your students walked out? You rush in and drop your bag in amazement. There are your students. They've taken roll, written the schedule on the board, pulled out their books, and begun their morning silent reading. In the corner, two students are helping your weakest reader. A few look up to wish you good morning.

These are moments when we who are teachers stand back and say, "They understand," when it is evident that children are *internalizing* what we have worked to teach them. Character education is about helping students internalize virtue so that they are able and willing to make wise choices and act on them when the mentors in their lives—such as parents and teachers—are not around.

The Internalizing Virtue Framework

The Internalizing Virtue Framework is an instructional and schoolwide framework that can help educators be more thoughtful and less haphazard in their efforts to educate for character. Built on the belief that character formation is a lifelong enterprise, the Internalizing Virtue Framework illustrates how we can help students move from an awareness of virtue and good character to the internalization of those habits that constitute good character. Exhibit 2.1 is a graphic representation of the framework. (See Appendix C, "Internalizing Virtue: An Instructional and Schoolwide Framework," for a reproducible depiction of the framework that incorporates Exhibits 2.1 and 2.2 and the following definitions.)

In the process of internalizing virtue, awareness, understanding, action, and reflection all play a part.

1. *Awareness* is raised as educators and others explain and define virtues, as a means of building a common language and shared character goals for the school community. Students become aware that respect, kindness, and diligence, for example, matter when teachers use these words and remind students of the importance of these virtues to both their intellectual and their personal development.

2. *Understanding* virtue is that "Aha!" moment for a student when he or she realizes that living virtuously and making wise choices contributes

EXHIBIT 2.1

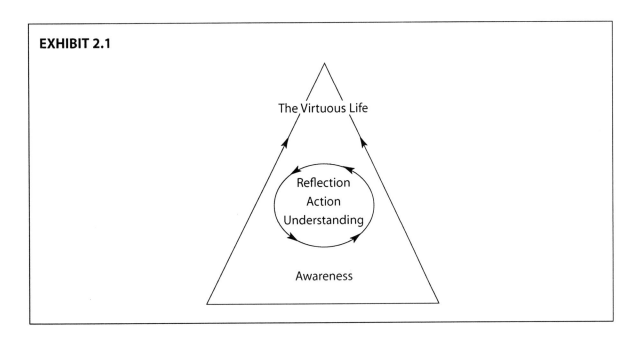

to personal happiness and the happiness of others. Understanding is enlightened through stories, poetry, images, music, film, and examples of lives past and present. Understanding heightens students' desire to lead a virtuous life; to use their time, talent, and energy well; and to make wise choices.

3. *Action* enables us to build good habits. We learn by doing. As Aristotle noted, "[Men] become builders by building and lyre-players by playing the lyre; so too we become just by doing just acts . . . brave by doing brave acts."[2] Action is about *putting virtue into practice.*

4. *Reflection* involves thinking about what we have done (a thoughtful examination of actions). Was it a good or a bad decision? Why? What would we do differently next time? Reflection helps us develop the self-knowledge essential to internalizing virtue. It *cultivates moral reasoning.*

Virtues, once again, are those good habits of mind, heart, and action that *dispose us to choose and act well.* Fostering virtue is at the heart of character education.

Internalizing virtue isn't just about acquiring a set of habits. It's about gradually gaining wisdom—acting and then reflecting on what we've done, learning from our mistakes, and coming to a greater understanding of how to live a life shaped by such qualities as compassion, respect, and honesty. This continuous cycle is graphically represented in Exhibit 2.2.

Our understanding informs our actions, our actions give us reason to reflect, and these reflections strengthen our understanding of virtue and our commitment to act accordingly.

Using the Internalizing Virtue Framework

Many educators have found the Internalizing Virtue Framework helpful as they educate for character through the curriculum, through classroom man-

---

EXHIBIT 2.2

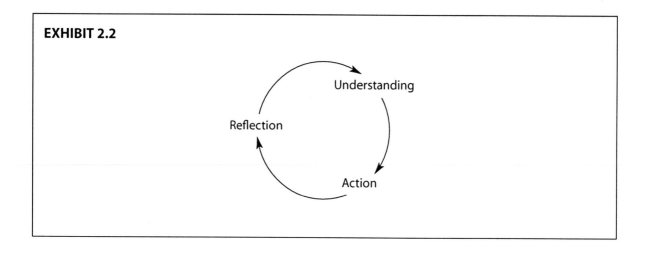

Understanding

Reflection

Action

agement, and through schoolwide initiatives. Here are some practical checklists to help you apply the framework in these areas and begin your strategic planning. Items that cannot be checked off should be treated as activities to be accomplished soon.

When you use the curriculum to educate for character, periodically complete Checklist 2.1 as an aid to curriculum development.

When using the framework to improve classroom management and climate, periodically complete Checklist 2.2.

Many schools new to character education rely heavily on *awareness* (for example, putting up banners and announcing the virtues the school emphasizes) but are less purposeful in helping students *understand* the virtues,

---

STRATEGIC PLANNING CHECKLIST 2.1

Curriculum Development

_____ I am *aware* of the virtue or the themes related to living virtuously (or not so virtuously) that I would like to lift into focus in a particular lesson or unit. I am using appropriate language that will help my students become *aware* of the definition and importance of this virtue. (Note that students can learn from bad examples as well as good. Sometimes drawing character flaws into focus can inspire a greater appreciation for virtue.)

_____ I have found stories, photographs, poems, biographies, history lessons, and other materials that will help students *understand* this virtue and bring it to life. I have determined how I can encourage students to think about and discuss the themes presented.

_____ I have planned an activity that will let students put what they are learning *into practice.*

_____ I give my students an opportunity to *reflect* on their actions and choices as well as those choices represented in the curriculum. I give them the opportunity to reflect on what they have learned, through writing or discussion.

STRATEGIC PLANNING CHECKLIST 2.2

Classroom Management

_____ Students are *aware* of the expectations and rules of the school.

_____ Students *understand* what it means, specifically, to act respectfully and responsibly at school.

_____ Teachers work together to help students *act* wisely in all areas of the school, and there are consequences for negative behavior.

_____ Teachers and students have occasion to *reflect* on specific behaviors and the overall climate of the school.

act upon them, and *reflect* upon their actions. Some schools are strong in *action* (for example, student-to-student tutoring and service activities) but provide few opportunities for students to *reflect* on what they have done and why. When using the framework to analyze the strengths and weaknesses of your school's character education efforts, periodically complete Checklist 2.3.

▶ Key Thoughts

In order for character education to be effective, we must engage the whole person: that is, we must engage and develop students' habits of mind, heart, and action. It is not enough simply to be *aware* of certain virtues. In order to internalize habits of mind, heart, and action, students must also *understand* and be compelled by the importance of these virtues to their everyday lives as students. Then they must be encouraged to routinely *practice* these virtues and to *reflect* on their choices and behaviors.

▶ Discussion and Reflection Activity

You can gain a better appreciation of the processes required to internalize virtue by answering this question:

- Think about how you learned a new skill, from dividing fractions to playing the piano. How did the concepts of awareness, understanding, action, and reflection come into play? If you play a musical instrument, for example, did you learn by simply becoming *aware* of certain principles and techniques, or did you need to *understand* them, *act* on them, and *reflect* on your progress? Who or what inspired you to persist?

▶ Best Practice Story

In a math class one day a middle school teacher confiscated a two-page note that a student had obviously been working on for some time. After class the teacher asked to meet with her after school. Before the meeting the teacher

---

STRATEGIC PLANNING CHECKLIST 2.3
Schoolwide Initiatives

_____ The school community has identified its strengths and weaknesses in character education.

_____ The school community has identified different strategies teachers and staff can employ to raise awareness, to foster understanding, to make time for reflection, and to encourage action.

_____ The school community has a plan for becoming strong in areas that are currently comparatively weak.

read the note and discovered that this bright young woman, popular with both peers and teachers, had been cruelly maligning one of the less popular girls in the class, a girl who was extremely self-conscious about being overweight. The sheer meanness of the note and the obvious cattiness it revealed were both alarming and disappointing to the teacher. When the offending student arrived, she was visibly ashamed and upset. The teacher simply said, "I read your note about Jennifer," and the girl dissolved into tears. A sober but fruitful discussion ensued. The young woman's shame turned to resolve when she acknowledged that she would be devastated if others were to talk about her in such brutal terms and, even worse, alienate her from her peers as a consequence. For the remainder of the school year, she not only stopped her cattiness toward this student but actually sought out ways to make her feel genuinely included among the note writer's own friends.

It sometimes takes a startling event like this to awaken students to the disharmony in their lives. All too often, students exhibit discordant responses. They may weep bitterly at the cruel injustice they see in a film or read in a story but turn right around at recess and bully the classmate who can't sink a basketball or taunt the classmate who stutters. Teachers have numerous opportunities throughout the school year to help students see where they can take steps toward developing virtue.

This student was not immediately aware of the meanness of her actions. The teacher's willingness to call her on her behavior drew its ugliness into sharp relief. The student was now able to understand the gravity and impact of her note writing. Through conversation with the teacher she was prompted to reflect on what she had done and why it was wrong. By taking determined action, she was able to turn this negative experience into an opportunity to befriend the person she had formerly criticized.

Key Principles for a Community of Virtue

How do you build a community of virtue? What does it take to change the culture of a school? To begin with, schools that excel at character education are able to state with confidence *who they are* and *what they stand for.* These shared ideals and principles serve as their social glue.

In the next four sections you will find a series of key principles that offer steps school staff can take to determine who they are as a school community and what that community stands for. These principles are organized around the four parts of the Internalizing Virtue Framework: raising awareness, inspiring understanding, developing habits of action, fostering reflection. Each section also includes a strategic planning checklist that staff can use to identify and put in place the elements needed to implement the framework.

Raising Awareness for Your Character Education Initiative

Take a team approach. In effective schools, implementing character education is the prerogative not of a single person but of a committed team. Therefore, raising awareness begins with forming a committee, task force, or leadership team, making sure that it is representative of the school and community. It is important that the members of this committee work closely with the entire school community throughout all stages of the planning process (see Checklist 2.4).

Form partnerships with the home. Invite parents to collaborate with teachers in a joint effort to help students acquire virtue and develop integrity. Schools need both the commitment and the trust of parents if they are to help children become morally responsible. Parents and teachers must work together to help students understand what it means to take pride in their work and to be personally accountable for what they choose to do or not to do. Parents and teachers can also jointly assist students in developing such intellectual virtues and skills as diligence, concentration, listening, planning, and organizing.

Identify the school's core virtues. Earlier you answered four questions to identify virtues important to your school. Now the members of the representative committee, task force, or leadership team should perform that exercise together and then go on to select the core virtues the school community wants to emphasize, using Worksheet 2.1 as a guide.

Get feedback. Most schools invite teachers, parents, and key community leaders to participate in identifying the final list of core virtues. For example, a school might send out a survey with a list of twenty virtues, asking each recipient to circle the five he or she believes are most important. The school community then uses this input in selecting three to six virtues as the core virtues. Note that a longer list of core virtues does not necessarily make a school's character education effort stronger. Some schools focus on only two or three virtues. Having a small number of core virtues makes it easier for teachers, parents, and students to develop a common vocabulary and communicate effectively about the school's expectations.

One caveat: do not let the process of arriving at a limited list of virtues limit your school's vision for helping students achieve both academic and character excellence. A set of core virtues provides orientation, a set of aspirations, not an endpoint. The ancient debate about the unity of the virtues (is virtue a whole or can it be considered in separate parts?) is relevant here.

WORSHEET 2.1

Identifying Core Virtues

1. Look at the virtues listed in Exhibit 1.2, and answer these questions:

   • Which of these virtues do you think your school is currently teaching?

   • Which virtues would you like to emphasize more deliberately schoolwide?

   • Which of these virtues work in concert with the academic goals of your school?

   • Which of these virtues support music, physical education, social interaction, and extracurricular activities?

2. Create a master list of virtues by combining everyone's answers. Alternatively, create a master list of potential core virtues through a group brainstorming activity.

3. Identify the three, five, or ten virtues that the group wants to prioritize. They should be the virtues most consistent with the identity and purpose of the school community, the ones that specify those intellectual and moral habits the group would like to see practiced by all the members of the school, the ones that define the character traits the school community hopes its graduates will possess.

4. Brainstorm answers to the following questions. (The ideas in Appendices F and G may be helpful here. Appendix F, "Virtue in Action: A K–8 Guide," suggests different ways specific virtues might be lived out in different grades. Appendix G, "Helping Younger Students Understand the Virtue of Respect," a similar guide, is designed specifically for young children and looks at one virtue in detail.)

   • How can these virtues be lived in our school?

   • How can we weave these virtues into classroom and schoolwide expectations?

   • If we do not make the effort to teach and model these virtues, what will be the consequences for our school community and our students?

The experience of the authors is that the development of one virtue or one set of virtues generally leads to the development of good character overall.

Review the mission statement. Revisit your school's mission statement. Does it articulate shared principles and ideals, such as *who we are* and *what we stand for*? Revise it to reflect the centrality of good character in academic and personal development.

Conduct a formal launch. Introduce the school's character education initiative at a formal assembly for the entire school community. Along with parents, school, political, community, and religious leaders can be invited to celebrate this new effort. Design the event to acquaint the community with your school's core virtues, mission statement, policy revisions, and other initiatives pertaining to character education.

▶ Key Thoughts

Forming a team or committee that is representative of the school and community is the first important step toward building a community of virtue at your school. Once this team is formed, work together to identify and select your school's core virtues. Revisit your school's mission statement, and make sure that these core virtues are reflected in it. Raise awareness of the core virtues by conducting a formal launch.

▶ Discussion and Reflection Activities

Parents, teachers, and school community members appreciate initiatives that support the twin goals of helping students develop academically and personally. Foster this appreciation through these activities:

- Discuss how your next celebration of character education in the school could demonstrate the ways that it supports the school's academic goals and mission.

- Invite parents and community members to speak on the importance of embracing a noble vision not only for students' performance but also for the kinds of persons we all hope the students will become.

▶ Best Practice Stories

In a series of evening meetings at Hilltop Elementary School in Lynnwood, Washington, parents responded positively to the idea of the school's focusing on character education. Families and community members worked side-by-side with teachers to come up with a set of core values that everyone could agree on, such as honesty and caring, and the journey began. Parents continue to be actively involved with Hilltop Elementary through the Parent Connection program, which provides advice, support, and knowledge about teaching values to children at home.

STRATEGIC PLANNING CHECKLIST 2.4

Awareness

_____ We have defined a vision and mission for our school that is shared by students, parents, and faculty.

_____ This vision and mission captures who we are and what we stand for.

_____ We have identified core virtues and defined them both conceptually and operationally in grade-appropriate language.

_____ We are taking deliberate and effective steps to help everyone understand the core virtues, desire to embody them, and become committed to them.

_____ We have developed a rubric illustrating what these core virtues look like in action. (See, for example, Columbine Elementary's rubrics in Appendix H.)

_____ We have a leadership group (or a committee or task force) that includes staff, students, parents, and community members and that guides the ongoing planning and integration of character education into the school community.

Teachers and staff at Longfellow Elementary School in Hastings, Nebraska, knew that they wanted to improve their school's climate and at the same time help their students form the enduring habits common to responsible members of society. A group of ten teachers set out to learn everything they could about character education. After selecting four core virtues—responsibility, compassion, integrity, and respect—they began raising awareness.

Joy White, a sixth-grade teacher, remembers that initial summer: "We started by looking through current articles. We designed posters, looked through published materials that supported those traits [the core virtues], designed a calendar for the year, and created a curriculum guide with activities. We also planned assemblies and staff development."

By the end of the summer the diligent committee was able to put something into every teacher's hand. It was a start, and soon interest grew. "These days," says Principal DeEtte Brasfield, "the four character traits govern everything in our school." (Exhibit 2.3 presents a sample calendar for teaching virtue throughout the school year.)

Fostering Understanding of Core Virtues

In helping teachers, staff, and students to understand the school's core virtues, follow these steps (see Checklist 2.5):

Determine what the school is already doing. Find ways for everyone in the school community to recognize what the school is already doing to foster

EXHIBIT 2.3

Benjamin Franklin Classical Charter School Character Education Calendar

Month	Core Virtue	Related Topics for Classroom Discussion
September	Justice	• Friendship • Respect for adults and peers
October	Temperance	• Order (staying organized; putting things away) • Courtesy and good manners
November	Prudence	• Gratitude • Honesty
December	Justice	• Respect for the dignity of others • Responsibility for the needs of others • Compassion and kindness
January	Fortitude	• Hope and optimism • Courage • Goal-setting
February	Temperance	• Patience • Obedience
March	Prudence	• Integrity (being true to your best self) • Humility (caring less about who's right and more about what's right)
April	Justice	• Generosity (giving without expecting anything in return) • Loyalty
May	Fortitude	• Citizenship and sacrifice • Perseverance
June	(Choose your focus)	• Ideas: heroes from history; local heroes, friendship revisited, and so forth

Useful Definitions for Teachers

Justice. Respect and responsibility for the well-being of others; fairness

Temperance. Mastering ourselves and our impulses for the sake of the happiness of those around us; moderation; acting the right way at the right time

Fortitude. Personal courage in the face of obstacles; persevering

Prudence. Sound judgment; making wise choices; thoughtfulness

Source: Reprinted by permission of the Benjamin Franklin Classical Charter School.

There are three things I live by. These three things have only been there for a few years, but I hear and see them every day: "Purpose, Pride, and Performance." Purpose—the word taht reminds me of why I am here and what I have to accomplish. Pride—what makes me stand tall each time I hear my name. Performance—the actions I take to move forward in my life. I have had four years at Mountain Pointe High School to live by these vows, and they have definitely made me a better person. I may not be a "perfect" role model, but I feel I have accomplished more at this school than I have anywhere else.
—STUDENT AT MOUNTAIN POINTE HIGH SCHOOL, PHOENIX, ARIZONA

character development. For example, teachers might look at the list in Appendix D, "100 Ways to Bring Character Education to Life," and star all the good habits the school community is already practicing. The seven strategic planning checklists in this chapter and the three-part survey reproduced in Appendix K are also excellent tools for sparking discussion of and reflection on your school's current policies and initiatives.

Identify ways to help teachers prepare. Teachers will need additional content and training so that they are more confident and competent in character education. What education and training will the school provide? How will in-service training be structured? What orientation will new teachers receive?

Provide information and resources to parents. Parents will need information and resources to help them understand the school's goal of fostering both academic and character excellence and to support them in their efforts at home. What materials will the school provide for parents?

Identify the natural tie-ins between the curriculum and the core virtues. Character education cannot be accomplished in isolation; it must be integrated into content and into all the learning experiences throughout the school day. Character and virtue are not disciplines or subjects to be studied separately from math, science, literature, and foreign language. Good habits of mind, heart, and action are nurtured and cultivated through the context of a rich and engaging curriculum. (See Chapter Four for ideas on integrating character education into the curriculum.)

▶ Key Thoughts

In order to commit themselves to character education, students, parents, teachers, and administrators must understand how a school's core virtues contribute to personal and academic growth and success.

▶ Discussion and Reflection Activities

To work further on the process of understanding virtues, use these activities to consider how you have arrived at your own understanding:

- Take one minute to list five classes, lectures, or talks that have had a positive impact on who you are. Next take one minute to list five individuals who have had a positive impact on your life. Then discuss what this exercise has illustrated. (It is typically easier to identify individuals. Our character is shaped more by persons and relationships than by formal classes. In many instances the classes people list in this exercise turn out to have been influential not only because of their content but also because of the individuals who taught them.)

- Put a star next to the names of three of the persons you listed. Discuss the virtues these individuals possess.

Putting Core Virtues into Action

In order to put the school's core virtues into action, the committee, task force, or leadership team can follow these steps (see Checklist 2.6):

Involve staff. In addition to teachers, include library, custodial, administrative, and cafeteria staff and also volunteers and bus drivers. Their work, example, and daily involvement with students should foster character development. For example, bus drivers should insist on courteous behavior. Cafeteria workers should expect students to clean up after themselves. Librarians can work with teachers to feature books that inspire students.

Involve students. Make sure students know that the school counts on their insights, feedback, example, and leadership in sustaining a community of virtue. Engage them in creating classroom constitutions and defining character goals.

Integrate extracurricular activities. Athletics, performing arts, and clubs all provide opportunities for students to practice the school's core virtues. Students need to see that there is a purpose larger than fun and games behind these activities—the purpose of helping them develop good habits and good character. The language of virtue and high expectations should be maintained in all the school's sponsored activities, events, and field trips.

Present opportunities for service. Take a look at your school's service projects. Are you making a specific link between service and character as you plan these initiatives? Do students know why the school is collecting food for the homeless or visiting the elderly? To meet a need, yes, but also to give the students and adults practice in developing certain virtues such as generosity, responsibility, and altruism.

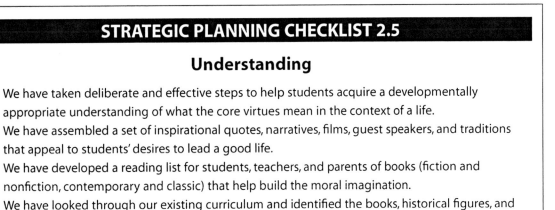

STRATEGIC PLANNING CHECKLIST 2.5

Understanding

_____ We have taken deliberate and effective steps to help students acquire a developmentally appropriate understanding of what the core virtues mean in the context of a life.

_____ We have assembled a set of inspirational quotes, narratives, films, guest speakers, and traditions that appeal to students' desires to lead a good life.

_____ We have developed a reading list for students, teachers, and parents of books (fiction and nonfiction, contemporary and classic) that help build the moral imagination.

_____ We have looked through our existing curriculum and identified the books, historical figures, and topics that tie in naturally with the virtues we hope to cultivate in our school.

Examine school traditions. Take a look at your school's traditions. Do they promote and reinforce the core virtues? Are there any events or behaviors that the school should develop into traditions?

Monitor behavior. Students will quickly become disillusioned if teachers preach about respect but turn a blind eye to harassment in the halls. Do students know how they are expected to behave in school? Is vulgar language prohibited? Is the dress code clear, fair, enforceable, and enforced? Are the tardy and attendance policies clear and enforced? Do teachers apply consistent and fair consequences? What help is available to students who are at risk?

▶ Key Thoughts

Putting character education into action involves the entire school community. Core virtues must be integrated not only into the school's curriculum but also into sports, performing arts, other extracurricular activities, and school traditions. Core virtues must also be reflected in school policies and in the ways that certain behaviors are corrected or enforced.

▶ Discussion and Reflection Activity

To focus on virtue in action in your school, conduct this activity:

- Ask a group of faculty and staff to choose one of the school's core virtues and then brainstorm the initiatives and habits of service students could undertake to develop that virtue. Once the group has generated a large list, it can choose another virtue and begin again. This time, people might identify the different actions students could undertake at home, at school, and in the community.

STRATEGIC PLANNING CHECKLIST 2.6

Action

_____ Our academic curriculum (lessons and units) gives students the opportunity to engage in good habits of heart, mind, and action.

_____ We have integrated our school's core virtues into the traditions, expectations, and extracurricular activities of the school.

_____ We have made our core virtues a part of the culture of the classroom and the culture of the school as a whole.

_____ We help students develop the habits of study, work, and collaboration they need to succeed in school.

_____ We have set clear expectations about the ways students will engage in moral action both in and outside the classroom.

_____ We make an effort to increase parental involvement in character education.

▶ Best Practice Stories

At Newsome Park Elementary School in Newport News, Virginia, each student stays with the same teacher for a two-year *loop*. In the K–1 loop, students work with senior citizens. In grades 2 and 3, the children work with the Department of Social Services on the Adopt-a-Family program, providing clothing, school supplies, and encouragement to families in need. Grade 4 and 5 students "adopt" a ward at the nearby Veterans Administration hospital. "Just watching the children in the quadriplegic ward at the VA hospital, you can see they are learning kindness and courage," says Principal Peter Bender.

Last Wednesday, the eleven-year-olds taught the latest dance craze to their buddies, who, despite some arthritic aches, were burning up the dance floor. This week the seniors will turn the tables by teaching their young friends some moves from the Big Band era. Unusual? Not for the middle school students at the Talent House Private School, grades Pre-K to 8, in Fairfax, Virginia.

After reading Mitch Albom's *Tuesdays with Morrie,* a chronicle of Albom's weekly visits with a beloved college professor who was dying, the students, along with their literature teacher, decided to adopt some seniors of their own and make the experience a character education project. Every other week the young students eagerly walk across the grounds of their campus and enter the doors of a neighboring assisted-living retirement community for their Wednesdays with Seniors parties. Inside, smiles break out on the faces of young and old, and the fun begins. Stories and scrapbooks are shared, games are played, and memories are created. Students then reflect on each session in their written journals and participate in a video journal.

"The activities vary, but the result is always the same. Everyone involved benefits from warm and caring interactions that come from the heart and stem from a value system based on respect for every generation," observes Marcia L. Wiggins, the school's director of education.

To make behavioral expectations explicit to parents, teachers, and administrators, the Character Education Committee at Traut Core Knowledge School in Fort Collins, Colorado, created a handbook titled *Door-to-Door.* The eighteen-page document describes the school's philosophy of discipline and also details appropriate conduct from "the moment the students open their front door in the morning to join a carpool to when they return home later that day."

"We are very specific and clear," says Principal Art Dillon. "Here is what character looks like in the carpool. Here is how to show kindness when you are lining up outside. This is how to enter the classroom in an appropriate way." The committee wanted to alert adults to what living the twelve traits that are the school's core virtues looks like, in order to establish a consistent set of behavioral standards.

In addition, Dillon notes that the handbook "reinforces our belief that parents are the first and primary educators of their students. This gives parents both responsibility and tools. We are secondary to the parents in teaching character. We are here to reinforce the character education that has been done at home."

Taking Time to Reflect on One's Progress

Teachers and staff need structured opportunities to think about their work on character education. To help the school community reflect on its school's character goals, consider making such reflection a priority item in regularly scheduled faculty-staff meetings (see Checklist 2.7).

Consider what is being done well. Begin by reflecting on what your school is doing right in the four areas of the Internalizing Virtue Framework. These four questions can focus the discussion: What virtues or character traits do we as a school focus on specifically and effectively? What are we already doing to help students understand the meaning of these virtues? What are we already doing to help students practice these virtues? (Think about service opportunities, behavioral policies, extracurricular events, and so on.) What are we already doing to help students think about these virtues and reflect on their own choices and the choices of others?

Consider improvements. After reflecting on what your school is doing right, discuss and assess how it might do better. These questions can guide you: How can we integrate the core virtues into our teaching and professional development? In what tangible, visible ways can our professional and social relationships with colleagues, students, and parents reflect the principles of character we hope to instill in our students? How can we consistently illustrate, practice, and demand from our students academic and personal excellence? What opportunities can we foster for moral reflection during formal and informal classroom activities? How can the mentoring program be revised to support the core virtues and allow teachers to share their ideas, concerns, and successes with each other? How can we refine classroom observations and evaluations as vehicles for discussing the moral implications of teaching and learning?

Conduct relevant evaluation. Some teachers and administrators like to begin evaluation by seeking hard-and-fast data: academic achievement scores, attendance records, number of disciplinary actions, responses from student surveys. However, a more important part of evaluation is to return to your school's mission statement and core virtues and to reflect on your school's ethos and where your school is heading as a community. For example, take a look at the condition of the school grounds, the tenor of schoolwide events, the atmosphere in the cafeteria, the language and social interactions in the hallways, the state of the lavatories—to what extent do these represent who you in the school community are and what you stand for? (Appendix K contains a three-part survey that can be completed by teachers, students, and parents to assess the school environment.)

▶ Key Thoughts

Schools of character are able to state with confidence who they are and what they stand for. It is these shared ideals and principles that govern these schools' lives and serve as their social glue. Building a community of virtue requires a commitment to these shared ideals, ongoing reflection, understanding, and assessment.

▶ Discussion and Reflection Activity

A community of virtue is sustained and communicated through relationships of trust and respect. They are the connective tissue that binds together students, teachers, administrators, staff, and by extension, parents and community members.

- To take the moral pulse of your school environment, administer the survey of perceived school environment in Appendix K. Tailor the survey to suit your school's vision, mission, and core virtues.

STRATEGIC PLANNING CHECKLIST 2.7

Reflection

_____ We periodically reflect on our efforts to implement character education as well as on our own growth as character educators.

_____ We assess student progress in developing an understanding of and commitment to the qualities of good character.

_____ Students are given opportunities to set character goals and reflect upon their own actions and patterns of behavior.

_____ We help students grasp the reasons why some behaviors are right and others wrong.

_____ We have examined our curriculum to see what core virtues are embedded in the academic content.

_____ We invite students to reflect upon the decisions and habits of others, both good and bad, in film, history, literature, and current events.

_____ We encourage students to discuss and write about themes of character as these themes emerge from the academic curriculum.

▶ Best Practice Stories

At Excelsior Academy in San Diego, California, a private school for students in grades 4 to 12 who have learning disabilities, the staff are used to discussing the needs and accomplishments of their students. Every Wednesday, students are dismissed at 12:30, and the faculty enter _learning mode._ This time is dedicated to in-service training and curriculum development and to choosing the new _students of the week_—a task that keeps teachers focused on _all_ students, not just those in their individual homerooms. The staff also read books together and conduct Socratic seminars on their readings. Additionally, staff revisit the mission and vision of the school every two years to "make sure it's still working for us." When it comes to hiring, says Nance McGuire, co-director of Excelsior Academy, "Obviously, we look for dedicated individuals!"

During a discussion one month, teachers at Atlantis Elementary School in Cocoa, Florida, realized the students were having problems with being responsible. Too many students were not turning in quality homework. The teachers moved from a discussion of the problem to ideas for action. They decided to buy homework planners for the students in grades 3, 4, and 5 and teach the students how to use them. They then established both a schoolwide homework policy and grade-level procedures on how to respond to missing or poor quality homework. "All this came through reflection," says Vicki Mace, the school's principal. "We have become a caring staff through these reflections."

Chapter 3

Building a Community of Virtue

> The greater part of our happiness or misery depends upon our dispositions and not upon our circumstances. We carry the seeds of the one or the other about with us, in our minds, wherever we go.
>
> —MARTHA WASHINGTON, letter

> Much of what we have become as a nation is shaped in the schoolyard and classroom.
>
> —GERALD GRANT, *The World We Created at Hamilton High*

SCHOOL ABSORBS an enormous chunk of our children's lives. Beginning when they have barely moved from the Big Wheel to the tricycle and continuing on through their adolescence, children spend a vast amount of their waking hours in school. This chapter examines the influence schools wield, whether they intend to or not, and considers how that inescapable influence can be designed and channeled to support the development of good character.

The Impact of School on Character

Because we are social beings and forge our lives in a social context, the ethos of a school has both an inevitable and a potentially permanent impact on its students. Classroom and school environments give rise to a variety of social relationships: among students, teammates, and cast and choir members; among teachers, administrators, and staff; between students and bus drivers, cafeteria staff, and custodians. The connective tissue that sustains these relationships—whether it is trust or mistrust, encouragement or antagonism, fear or mutual respect—has a powerful character-shaping influence.

Students quickly pick up on the tacit values at work in their school community and build patterns of behavior around them. For example, on the one hand, survival skills are cultivated in environments where older children bully younger children. Manipulation and cheating are heightened in schools where rank in class and academic achievement are prized above all else.

On the other hand, a school with a strong moral ethos can draw out the very best in its students. When virtue and the opportunity to practice it resonate throughout the community—from the cafeteria to the playground and from the classroom to the faculty lounge—then virtue is practiced, taught, expected, and honored.

▶ Key Thoughts

Children and adolescents need adult tutelage not simply in algebra and agriculture. They especially need it to understand and acquire the strong moral habits that contribute to good character. Becoming a person of character is a developmental process requiring knowledge, effort, and practice. It takes support, example, encouragement, and sometimes inspiration. In short, it takes *character education.*

▶ Discussion and Reflection Activities

Increase your awareness of your school's influence on character by answering these questions:

- No school is without an ethos. How would you describe the ethos of your school?
- What words or phrases come to mind when you think of each of the following school areas and daily events:

  Cafeteria

  Lunch duty

  Dismissal

  Recess

  Girls' bathroom

  Boys' bathroom

  Your classroom

  Faculty room

  Main office

  Hallways

"There is definitely a change in the students since Brookside's focus on character education and relationship building has been in place. Kids are more able to take the perspective of someone else. That's important so they do not become so self-absorbed. They are coming to learn how their actions affect others as well as how they can help others."

—LYNN LISY-MACAN, principal, Brookside Elementary School, Binghamton, New York

▶ Best Practice Stories

Mound Fort Middle School in Ogden, Utah, has transformed its ethos by linking its efforts to improve literacy with a service program. Several years ago the faculty agreed that they needed to focus aggressively on reading because many of their students were illiterate. The school brought in reading specialists to train the teachers. In addition, students were trained to read aloud. Now students practice and share their reading skills each week by reading stories to the elderly in a local nursing home and to children in the neighboring elementary school. Not only have scores skyrocketed, says Principal Tim Smith, but also violence in the school has plummeted. Perhaps one of the most telling results of this schoolwide effort comes from a parent who was astounded to discover her previously television-addicted thirteen-year-old son reading to his little sister instead of watching his favorite shows.

Several years ago one veteran teacher at Bailey Gatzert Elementary School in Seattle, Washington, said that "the playground was like a battlefield." There has since been a radical improvement in student behavior and academic performance, due largely to the school's Four Promises program: everyone in the school community promises to act in a safe and healthy way, to respect the rights and needs of others, to treat all property with respect, and to take responsibility for learning.

It was not the Four Promises program alone that effected change. The administrators, teachers, and playground staff were also committed to teaching the children how to play fairly. Additionally, the in-school counseling and family support workers joined teachers and staff in constantly referring to the Four Promises. However, the key to the program's success was invoking notions of honor and commitment in the students; this tapped a deeper motivation than mere compliance with rules and regulations. When students feel responsibility for their school's ethos, teachers are not the ones who say, "We don't do that here!" Students will become invested in a world they help create.

It's the Little Things

The moral life of a community is made up of many little things, and a community of virtue attends to those little things. On the academic front, everything from helping students see the importance of finishing their work neatly, completely, and on time to teachers' keeping their word about quiz dates, deadlines, and grading criteria falls under the umbrella of the little things. Emphasizing the school's appearance is another constant invitation to grow in virtue. Hanging student work attractively, putting tables and chairs back where they belong, leaving the blackboard clean, and returning books to the library are among the long list of daily responsibilities that should be shared by everyone in the school community. Paying attention to the little things will also improve the moral ethos of a school community and foster pride in its members.

▶ Key Thoughts

It's been said that "success is the sum of detail," and in order for character education to work, schools need to pay attention to the little things that cumulatively make a big impression on students.

▶ Discussion and Reflection Activities

To start identifying the little things that matter, answer these questions and complete Checklist 3.1.

- What little things do teachers, staff, and students at your school practice doing well?

- What little things are being neglected at your school?

- If your school were to work on improving one little thing a month, what would be at the top of your list?

▶ Best Practice Story

At St. Leonard Elementary School in rural Maryland, the work of integrating the school's character traits, the Eight Great Traits, is not limited to classroom teachers. The media specialist, for example, gives a monthly Power

---

"Character Education is not a single course, a quick-fix program, or a slogan posted on the wall; it is an integral part of school life. The school must become a community of virtue in which responsibility, hard work, honesty, and kindness are modeled, taught, expected, celebrated, and continually practiced. From the classroom to the playground, from the cafeteria to the faculty room, the formation of good character must be the central concern."

—THE CHARACTER EDUCATION MANIFESTO

STRATEGIC PLANNING CHECKLIST 3.1

Little Things and Lesser Places

Use this checklist to evaluate and then improve the little things and lesser places that affect your school-wide character education initiative. Items that cannot be checked require attention.

The School Bus

_____ Bus drivers are treated as important members of the school community. For example, they are recognized at assemblies or thanked by parents, students, and staff.

_____ The school responds immediately to a problem on a bus by calling a meeting with the students involved and their parents.

_____ Bus drivers are supported and recognized by the school as character educators. They are encouraged to uphold the school's core virtues on the bus.

_____ Parents back the school and the bus driver when they are asked to speak with their child about misbehavior on the bus.

_____ Older students, in a Big Sister, Big Brother tradition, look out for new and younger students who are riding the bus for the first time.

_____ Students feel safe on the bus. (If not, why? Are these issues being addressed proactively?)

The Hallways

_____ Teachers and administrators make eye contact with students and greet them in the hallways.

_____ The hallways are clean and safe.

_____ The adults in the school make an effort to keep student work posted neatly.

_____ There is zero tolerance for vulgar language and gestures. Public displays of affection are not tolerated. These issues are discussed by faculty and staff with the aim of promoting a coherent character-building effort (not simply as disciplinary problems).

_____ The hallways are clear during class time. Adults circulate in the hallways, not as police agents but as reminders to students that the adults in the building care about where they are and how they are spending their time.

Study Halls

_____ Students are assigned adequate (and engaging) homework, so that they have something to do in study hall.

_____ Students are taught that using study halls well is an effective way to learn to manage their time and improve their study habits.

_____ Students are required to arrive in study hall with books, pens, papers, and necessary supplies.

_____ Students who want to work on a group project have a way to do so without distracting the rest of the class.

_____ Study hall monitors are alert to what the students are doing. They do not permit note writing or inappropriate magazines.

_____ Teachers discuss the issues and challenges of leading a quiet study hall. They have worked out a policy and expectations in keeping with the school's core virtues.

The Lavatories

_____ Bathrooms in the school are safe, clean, and in working condition (the doors are on their hinges, the lights and faucets work, and the windows open).

_____ There are adequate supplies of soap, paper towels, and toilet paper.

_____ The walls are not covered with graffiti. (Perhaps each class participates in a "bathroom beautification" project, scrubbing or repainting walls. Activities like this can conclude with a picnic, pizza lunch, or sundae party sponsored by the PTO.)

_____ Adults or responsible students properly monitor the bathrooms to ensure that smoking, gossip, vandalism, and other inappropriate activities are nipped in the bud.

The Playground

_____ The playground is an inviting and clean area in which students can play safely.

_____ A few games or sports are organized and overseen by older students or playground monitors to minimize exclusion and maximize student involvement.

_____ Teachers and monitors take time out to discuss positive and negative playground incidents (with individual students or the whole group, depending on the situation).

_____ Monitors and older students stop fights, foul language, and littering immediately.

_____ Different grade levels are assigned to clean up and spruce up an area of the playground as a class project.

The Cafeteria

_____ The school's core virtues and code of standards or expectations are posted in the cafeteria.

_____ Teachers and other adults in the school speak with students and visit tables for friendly conversation during lunchtime.

_____ Students are assigned jobs in the cafeteria on a rotating basis, taking the responsibility for such things as reminding classmates to throw their trash away, distributing drinks or lunches, sweeping the floor, wiping down tables, or pushing chairs back under the tables when lunchtime is over.

_____ Cafeteria monitors remind students to speak and act with courtesy and to wait their turn in line.

_____ There are logical consequences for serious misbehavior in the cafeteria.

Point presentation about one of the traits to all classes. The music teacher incorporates songs that exemplify the character traits. The school counselor teaches classroom lessons on the traits as they relate to resolving conflict, controlling anger, developing empathy, and communicating positively. In short, the entire staff has ownership of teaching character, recognizing that character and academics make strong partners. "Principals who see character education as an add-on are totally missing the boat," says Principal Ted Haynie. "Obviously, traits like responsibility and self-discipline transfer directly to academic performance."

Caring Enough to Correct Others

We live in an era of "positive thinking" and "warm fuzzies." It is also an era that underestimates the resilience and realism of youth. To build a community of virtue, we certainly need to take the time and the interest to offer a word of encouragement and sincere praise to our students (and colleagues) when it is warranted. But we also need to be ready to correct them—and to be skilled at doing so—and we must offer advice that will help them grow in virtue. Helping a student get an objective picture of the consequences of his or her rude behavior is not easy. Trying to do it entirely through positive comments is impossible. Appendix J, for example, displays the Benjamin Franklin Classical Charter School Discipline Reflection Form. A structured way to correct students, it assists them to reflect on poor choices and actions and to consider how they might behave better in the future.

▶ Key Thoughts

Character is usually developed in the context of relationships. A community of virtue is a composite of supportive relationships, in which adults take students—both *who they are* and *who they are becoming*—seriously.

▶ Discussion and Reflection Activities

To gain a clearer picture of the reasons for actively correcting student behavior, consider these questions:

- Think of a time someone cared enough to correct you. What effect did it have on you?

- What is the difference between constructive criticism and destructive criticism? Give examples of each.

- From your answers to the first two questions, what conclusions can you draw about appropriate ways to help students make good choices?

▶ Best Practice Story

They are the students no one else can handle. Some have been kicked out of not just one but many schools. Coming to Youth Opportunities Unlimited, a remarkable 7–12 school in San Diego, California, is their last chance before being assigned to a court-ordered school or being incarcerated. When Principal Willie Horton Jr. walks down the halls of his school, he has one question for his students: "Are you on track?" The school's core virtues are graphically displayed on a racetrack to reinforce this concept. If students are abiding by the core values, they are on track to be successful. If through

---

"People who take the time to criticize you are often, in my experience, the ones who love you the most."
—R. WASHINGTON JARVIS, Headmaster, Roxbury Latin School, Boston, Massachusetts

a poor decision they fall off track, they need to make amends and get themselves back in the race for success.

"I tell the students that they have the power," states Horton. "As long as you stay on track and adhere to core values, you will stay here. It's up to you. They understand the concept of staying on track: they know the rules of the race. When they come into my office, I say, 'Did you fall off track today?' I say, 'Do you want to get back on? What value did you violate?' Then we talk about the values, and we come up with a valid consequence."

Chapter 4

Cultivating Character Through the Curriculum

Laziness may appear attractive, but work gives satisfaction. Virtue is worth the effort.

—ANNE FRANK, *The Diary of a Young Girl*

You must know that there is nothing higher, or stronger, or sounder, or more useful afterwards in life, than some good memory, especially a memory from childhood, from the parental home. You hear a lot said about your education, yet some such beautiful, sacred memory, preserved from childhood, is perhaps the best education. If a man stores up many such memories to take into life, then he is saved for his whole life. And even if only one good memory remains with us in our hearts, that alone may serve some day for our salvation.

—FYODOR DOSTOEVSKY, *The Brothers Karamazov*

"I would ask you to remember this one thing," said Badger. "The stories people tell have a way of taking care of them. If stories come to you, care for them. And learn to give them away where they are needed. Sometimes a person needs a story more than food to stay alive. That is why we put these stories in each other's memory. This is how people care for themselves."

—BARRY LOPEZ, *Crow and Weasel*

WHERE DOES CHARACTER education fit into the curriculum? The simple answer is this: everywhere. This chapter discusses using the curriculum to develop moral literacy, moral imagination, and moral discourse and to foster moral integrity in ways that will endure beyond school walls.

Evaluating Your Curriculum's Emphasis on Good Character

Character education seeks to cultivate wisdom—the practical intelligence and moral insight we need to make good choices and lead our lives well. The curriculum can be a primary source of our shared moral wisdom. Stories, biographies, historical events, and reflections provide us with a guide to what it means to lead a good life and possess strong moral character. Schools can allow the moral themes that can be found in all subjects to surface, and we can treat these themes with as much seriousness as we treat learning how to write a paragraph or multiply fractions.

Appendix L, for example, offers an outline of invigorating a unit on the Great Depression with ideas about the virtues of courage and hope. Like all the curriculum outlines in this chapter and the appendices, it uses the Internalizing Virtue Framework to organize the classroom discussion and activities. (Also like the other outlines, it is not intended to describe all the content or lessons taught during the unit. Rather, it describes a few activities that draw out the unit's overarching theme.)

A good first step in character education is for teachers to determine what they are already doing to cultivate character through the curriculum. Then they can build on those existing elements to provide more opportunities for practicing virtue and for reflecting on one's actions. Worksheet 4.1 is a guide for these steps in curriculum planning. It follows the Internalizing Virtue Framework (Appendix C).

▶ Key Thoughts

If we want students to understand virtue, we must teach it. And this does not mean instituting a separate course. Awareness of and reflection on virtue must be infused throughout the curriculum.

▶ Discussion and Reflection Activities

To begin developing specific curriculum materials, divide teachers and administrators into either grade-level or subject-area teams to complete these activities:

- Review the responses to Worksheet 4.1 to identify the inherent moral lessons available in the curriculum's prescribed content and skills.

- Work together to develop and exchange lesson plans that tap the moral dimensions of a particular story, event, experiment, or topic. (Science teachers could ask themselves, for example, how a science lab session can become a character-building experience for students, fostering teamwork, responsibility, and intellectual honesty.)

WORKSHEET 4.1

Curriculum Development: Building on Existing Materials to Internalize Virtue

This worksheet may be usefully completed both by individual teachers and by teachers working together in subject area groups. It can be used to examine an entire curriculum or a single unit. Answer the questions for each of the four teaching goals through which teachers can help students internalize virtue.

1. **Building awareness.** Think about the core virtues you identified earlier.

    • What are some virtues (habits of mind, heart, and action) that your students need to develop?

2. **Inspiring understanding.** Think about your curriculum.

    • What narratives, books, history units, musical pieces, works of art, thought-provoking quotations, or other curricular materials and topics illustrate virtues or themes related to character and ethics?

    • How could you use this content to move and inspire students?

    • How could you use these examples and images to help students see the difference between good and bad choices?

3. **Developing habits of action** (helping students practice virtue and choose well). Think about your teaching and subject area.

    • What activities, behavioral expectations, or projects would invite students to practice these virtues more consistently?

    • How could you create opportunities for students to practice making and acting on good choices?

4. **Fostering reflection** (helping students analyze, judge, critique, and make distinctions). Think about your classroom activities.

    • What opportunities currently exist for students in your classroom to reflect on the difference between, for example, courage and recklessness, choice and impulse, a friend and an accomplice?

- What questions emerge from your curriculum that could help students explore the ethical dimensions and impact of individuals' choices?

- How could you structure projects, discussions, and writing assignments to help students develop habits of reflection, analysis, and good judgment?

▶ **Best Practice Stories**

Character education can be very effective when it is taught across the curriculum. Marion Intermediate School in rural South Carolina seeks to do this. For example, in teaching a unit on justice using a Native American Cinderella story titled *The Rough-Face Girl,* students might find synonyms for *justice* in the story (language arts). The class then might conduct a mock trial of the wicked stepmother in the story to determine justice in action (social studies); grow Native American plants (science); graph the number of brothers, sisters, stepsisters, and stepbrothers in the class (math); and design symbols that represent justice (art).

The material a school needs for character education can often be found in its existing curriculum. For example, when it opened, Traut Core Knowledge School adopted the curriculum designed by E. D. Hirsch, the author of *Cultural Literacy,* for the express purpose of providing students with a rich exposure to literature, math, science, history, art, and music. "By using the literature in the Core Knowledge sequence," says Principal Art Dillon, "we have a foundation for our character education program." To help teachers accomplish character education goals, the parents on the school's Character Education Committee launched an ambitious effort. They created a seventy-page Character Education Matrix, aligning the school's twelve character traits (core virtues) with the Core Knowledge literature and history sequence. For each reading selection from each grade, committee members created a grid, listing the chapters or scenes down the side and the twelve traits across the top. They then put a star in the appropriate cell when a chapter contained an example of the particular trait; they also put a no in the appropriate cell when a chapter contained an example of dishonesty or disrespect. The matrix took almost a year to complete, but after its distribution it became a resource for teachers as they planned their character education mini-lessons.

Developing Moral Literacy

As E. D. Hirsch's concept of cultural literacy suggests, a deliberate effort needs to be made in this country to promote moral literacy. One way we can make this effort is by incorporating the study of exemplary lives into our curricula. Young people need a meaningful frame of reference, and one way for them to create such a frame is by acquiring knowledge of individuals who bring the moral journey to life for them—people like Marie Curie, Mahatma Gandhi, Eleanor Roosevelt, and Nelson Mandela, for example. Becoming familiar with the lives of some of these extraordinary people can help counter the current widespread loss of heroes and moral ideals in the hearts and minds of our students.

In addition, we need not shy away from introducing students to the negative—to lives motivated by greed, selfishness, and hypocrisy. Persons of ignoble character also teach valuable lessons. However, it is important that we provide our students with balance and realism. If we tip the scale too far to the dark side, we run the risk of promoting moral skepticism and cynicism in our students.

Appendix M, "Developing Courage Through Sojourner's Example," presents an example of curriculum content for the fifth grade that concentrates on developing the virtue of courage through studying the extraordinary life of Sojourner Truth.

▶ Key Thoughts

It is important to expose students to the lives of fascinating people for whom virtue was far from boring and for whom the development of good character came with difficulty, mistakes, surprises, and turnarounds. These individuals' stories can make a lasting impression on the hearts and minds of students, nurturing their moral imagination and planting the seeds of aspiration.

▶ Discussion and Reflection Activities

Use the following questions and the concluding activity to prompt discussion about the advantages of learning about character from a life rather than a lesson:

- When you think of Harriet Tubman, Mahatma Gandhi, or George Washington, what choices and virtuous actions come to mind?

- How could study of these individuals' lives serve as the basis for a lesson or series of lessons on virtue? What literature could you use to spark student interest in one or more of these lives?

- How could you connect the lives of these individuals to the lives of your students?

- Identify an individual from history, literature, or film who has made an impact on your life, and analyze why he or she has had that impact.

▶ **Best Practice Story**

At Mountain Pointe High School in Phoenix, Arizona, students in Evan Anderson's writing class compose reflective essays on the subject of character. These are the suggested approaches for their essays:

- Is character important (especially for public figures), or are performance and skills all that matter?

- Focus on one person's character that you greatly admire. Reflect on the person, his or her character, and how it has influenced you.

- Have we, as a society, lost sight of the qualities that constitute character?

- Is character defined by universal qualities or does it depend on cultural setting, individual viewpoints, and so on?

- Reflect on a definitive moment in your life when your character was shaped or strengthened. How did it happen? What has been the effect or result?

Exciting the Moral Imagination

Young people can often be introduced imaginatively or vicariously to the importance of good character. The stories they hear and the art they explore have the power to transform them. As Louise Rosenblatt explains, "To enter a story, we must leave ourselves behind, and this it may be argued, is precisely what is needed to get a proper perspective on ourselves."[1] Good stories enlarge our students' minds and hearts. They help them shed their preoccupation with self and see what they have the potential to give or to do.

In addition, rich narratives, films, and music can help young people to develop empathy. We teach students to empathize by asking them probing questions and engaging them in activities that enable them to walk in someone else's shoes. Empathy connects us with others and allows us to experience incredible circumstances vicariously, such as Anne Frank's life in hiding. Such experiences can encourage students to resolve in the quiet of their hearts to elevate their lives by, for example, standing up for the threatened and the vulnerable.

Tapping the moral imagination also provides a setting, safely detached from students' own lives, where they can comfortably ask, What is the right thing to do? Students can more confidently ask this question of a character in literature or a figure in history than they can of themselves in their own situation; however, asking it of these others points students toward an understanding of good and bad choices, obligation and irresponsibility, integrity and hypocrisy. If this question is asked frequently of lives under study, students will eventually acquire the confidence to ask it of themselves and their peers.

Here is a series of questions and suggested activities the authors have used with K–12 teachers across subject areas to help them tap their students' moral imagination. These questions and activities may be used as prompts for reader-response exercises, journal writing, or in-class discussion.

- Which character in the book [or novel, play, biography, or other work] you are reading would you most like to be like? Did this character face a difficult challenge? How did he or she overcome it?

- Which of his or her character traits would you most like to have in a friend? Why?

- What have you learned most from your encounter with this character?

- Which character would you least like to be like? Why? What have you learned from this character?

- Identify and briefly describe your favorite or least favorite character in the book, and write either an original poem that captures the personality and qualities of this character or a journal entry from this character's point of view that chronicles his or her thoughts and reflections about a significant event or experience in the book.

- Write a letter to a friend that describes a memorable scene from the story. Be sure to explain why it was so memorable to you.

- Discuss something meaningful you have learned from this particular book. Be as specific as you can.

Even very young children can be introduced to ideas of good character through art and literature, as the list of useful picture books in Exhibit 4.1 demonstrates. Appendix N, "Envisioning Diligence," is a lesson plan for exploring ideas about diligence in one of these books.

EXHIBIT 4.1

Picture Books That Build the Moral Imagination

Respect

- *All the Places to Love*, Patricia MacLachlan
- *Great Uncle Albert Forgets*, Ben Schechter
- *The Ugly Duckling*, Hans Christian Anderson
- *The Little Match Girl*, Hans Christian Anderson
- *Chester's Way*, Kevin Henkes
- *Frederick*, Leo Lionni
- *Yussel's Prayer*, Barbara Cohen
- *Through Grandpa's Eyes*, Patricia MacLachlan
- *The Frog Prince*
- *The Rough-Face Girl*, Rafe Martin
- *Hansel and Gretel*
- *Molly's Pilgrim*, Barbara Cohen
- *Beauty and the Beast*

Integrity

- *The Empty Pot*, Demi
- *Honest Abe*, Evaline Ness
- *The Emperor's New Clothes*
- *Sam, Bangs, and Moonshine*, Evaline Ness
- *The Stonecutter: A Japanese Folktale*, Demi
- *The Tale of Peter Rabbit*, Beatrix Potter
- *The Adventures of Pinocchio*, adapted by Sue Kassirer
- *The Pied Piper of Hamelin*
- *Why Mosquitoes Buzz in People's Ears: A West African Tale*, Verna Aardema
- *The Gold Coin*, Alma Flor Ada
- *Matilda Who Told Such Dreadful Lies*, Hilaire Belloc
- *The Sabbath Lion*, Howard Schwartz
- *Daniel in the Lion's Den*
- *Old Turtle*, Douglas Wood

Kindness

- *Good Griselle*, Jane Yolen
- *The Pearl*, Helme Heine
- *Somebody Loves You, Mr. Hatch*, Eileen Spinelli
- *Frog and Toad Are Friends*, Arnold Lobel
- *Chrysanthemum*, Kevin Henkes
- *The Hating Book*, Charlotte Zolotow
- *Mufaro's Beautiful Daughters*, John Steptoe
- *The Queen's Necklace: A Swedish Folktale*, Jane Langton
- *The Emperor and the Kite*, Jane Yolen
- *Bub, or The Very Best Thing*, Natalie Babbitt
- *The Happy Prince*, Oscar Wilde
- *The Bicycle Man*, Allan Say
- *The Selfish Giant*, Oscar Wilde
- *The Velveteen Rabbit*, Margery Williams

Courage and Diligence

- *Miss Rumphius*, Barbara Cooney
- *Now One Foot, Now the Other*, Tomie dePaolo
- *Mike Mulligan and His Steam Shovel*, Virginia Lee Burson
- *The Tortoise and the Hare*
- *Alfie Gives a Hand*, Shirley Hughes
- *Cecil's Story*, George Ella Lyon
- *The Little Engine That Could*, Watty Piper
- *Silent Lotus*, Jeanne M. Lee
- *Brave Irene*, William Steig
- *The Boy Who Held Back the Sea*, Lenny Hort
- *Lon Po-Po: A Red Ridinghood Story from China*, Ed Young
- *It Could Always Be Worse*, Margot Zemach
- *The Lotus Seed*, Sherry Garland
- *Wagon Wheels*, Barbara Brenner
- *Peppe the Lamplighter*, Elisa Bartone
- *Hidden in the Sand*, Margaret Hodges
- *The Legend of the Bluebonnet*, Tomie dePaolo
- *A Chair for My Mother*, Vera Williams
- *How Many Days to America: A Thanksgiving Story*, Eve Bunting

Source: Developed by the Center for the Advancement of Ethics and Character at Boston University.

▶ Key Thoughts

Narrative and art have long served as profound teachers, helping us not only to identify models of vice and virtue but also to engage the larger questions: What makes life meaningful? What constitutes true happiness? What does it mean to be human? The right stories can ignite students' moral imagination, teach them empathy, and give them the courage to examine their own lives.

▶ Discussion and Reflection Activities

Identifying and discussing a book or film that made an impression on you is a helpful way to show students that reflection upon what they read and view can help them acquire wisdom.

- Think of a favorite book that you enjoy sharing with students. Reflect on discussions you have had or questions you have asked based on that story. Have students been able to use the story as a prompt for examining their own lives?

- What other stories could you use to prompt discussion about, for example, happiness, humanity, and empathy? How will you connect these ideas to the students' lives?

▶ Best Practice Story

In Sandy Juniper's American Studies class at Mountain Pointe High School, students read Arthur Miller's *The Crucible.* In a series of responsive writings, they consider such issues as right and wrong versus legal and illegal; a person's responsibility to self versus his or her responsibility to the community; and the effects of fear, hysteria, and prejudice. Using cooperative learning techniques, they then relate Miller's play to readings describing the Holocaust and McCarthyism.

Stimulating Moral Discourse Both Within and Beyond the Classroom

Socrates, the great teacher and lover of wisdom, used dialogue to pursue the truth. Picking up on this, excellent teachers know that thoughtful dialogue is not only a powerful way to investigate a topic but also a wonderful way to foster friendships in a classroom. When students become engaged in moral discourse, they learn to take moral themes seriously and to take others seriously. Moral discourse in school has at least three incarnations: (1) class discussions (about history, literature, or science for example), (2) class meetings, and (3) private conversations between the teacher and small groups of students or individual students.

In addition to thoughtful discussions in the classroom, conversations beyond the classroom can have a dramatic effect on the moral development of our students. A powerful way to promote such discourse is to assign intergenerational interview projects. In a unit on World War II, for instance, students can be assigned to interview a relative or friend who is a veteran of the war or who was a civilian during wartime. Many of the children the authors have known who have conducted such interviews have returned to class saying they had never before had a conversation like that with this relative or friend. Others are enormously impressed with what it took to endure the challenges of everyday life during World War II.

▶ Key Thoughts

We cannot overestimate the power of conversation to foster character both within and beyond the classroom. Encourage dialogue on moral issues between your students and between students and members of the community.

▶ Discussion and Reflection Activities

Well-structured class meetings provide opportunities for moral discourse. One way to encourage reflective conversation is to begin the meeting with a thoughtful question and then provide students with ten minutes to write about their ideas before opening the discussion. For example, ask students to "consider the examples of respect and disrespect you've seen at school this year. What can we do to make this classroom [or the hallway, or the lunch room] a more consistently respectful environment?"

- Brainstorm questions that would be appropriate to use with your students to initiate reflective conversation. Questions might focus on the school's core values in relation to students' experience in the school or in relation to the curriculum.

▶ Best Practice Story

At Excelsior Academy in San Diego, California, a fourth- through twelfth-grade school for students with learning disabilities, several classes conduct Socratic seminars. Socratic seminars are based on the Socratic method. Socrates helped introduce the notion that much of teaching lies not in the telling but in the questioning. Questioning allows students to work through ideas themselves, with guidance from the teacher. Excelsior students are given specific guidelines such as these to help them draw the most from these seminars:

- Refer to the text when needed during the discussion. A seminar is not a test of memory. You are not "learning a subject"; you are aiming at understanding ideas, values, and issues.

- Do not stay confused; ask for clarification.

- Do not participate if not prepared. A seminar should not be a bull session.

- Listen carefully. Talk to each other, not just to the teacher.

- You are responsible for the seminar, even if you don't know it or admit it.

Helping Students Develop Integrity or Maturity

Up to this point this chapter has discussed the curriculum as a source and carrier of our moral heritage. Identifying great lives, cultivating moral imagination and empathy, and raising moral questions, however, speak only to half of what the curriculum—in the hands of thoughtful and engaging teachers—can do to promote character education. The other half of what curriculum can do is to encourage our students' movement toward moral integrity.

Students who learn to slide by or beat the system do not acquire the habits of mind and character they need for moral integrity. Instead they acquire the skills of manipulation and perhaps even subterfuge, which may eventually become injurious to themselves and others. Therefore we need to be wary of miss-the-mark character education (see Exhibit 4.2), which takes as its central focus, not virtue and ways of incorporating virtue into one's life, but self-esteem, rewards and punishments, moral dilemmas, or social skills.

Virtue is difficult. As Aristotle explains (see Chapter One and Exhibit 1.3), it takes a settled disposition to habitually choose what is best and right between two extremes (to habitually choose, for example, friendliness over either rudeness or obsequiousness; courage over either cowardice or recklessness). Our method in teaching math, science, gym, or any other subject has to include the daily, ongoing effort to help our students apply themselves in such a way that they will eventually come to choose well, to internalize such virtues as self-discipline, perseverance, diligence, and responsibility. In this way we will equip them with the inner strength they need to live well each day for the rest of their lives.

Self-esteem and the joy of achievement are the fruits, not the roots, of these virtues. Furthermore, moral integrity will enable our students not only to live well for themselves but also to capably judge and critique those customs, social institutions, and laws that hinder both their own and others' individual and social development.

EXHIBIT 4.2

Miss-the-Mark Education

Self-Esteem

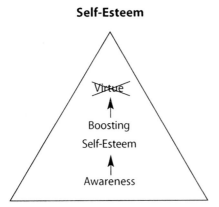

Emotional gratification becomes the end of this brand of "character education," rather than a diligent effort to become a better person. Self-esteem is a fruit of virtue, not the root of virtue.

Although praise has a place in the classroom, we cannot let character education stop there. Students need to know we care enough to challenge them to strive for excellence of mind and character. *What's missing? A conception of the virtuous life.*

Rewards and Punishments

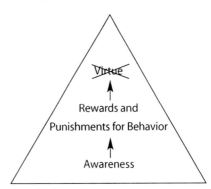

The desire to avoid punishment or recieve a reward can quickly become the motivation for "good behavior." This motivation is extrinsic rather than instrinsic.

We need to acknowledge virtuous actions. Similarly, we need to curb misbehavior with appropriate consequences. However, educating for virtue does not stop here. We need to help students desire to lead a good life for its own sake. *What's missing? Understanding.*

Moral Dilemmas

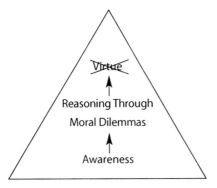

Reasoning through moral dilemmas does not necessarily lead to moral action. The goal of this exercise is to engage students in a lively discussion and have them come up with the "best" answer or smoothest argument.

It is useful to invite older students to reason through moral questions; it heightens their awareness of the moral dimension of their lives. Sharp reasoning alone, however, does not necessarily lead students to practice virtue. *What's missing? Action.*

Social Skills

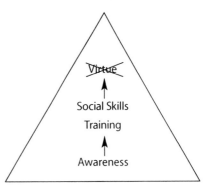

When social savvy becomes the motivation for good action instead of a genuine interest in living a virtuous life, students may find it difficult to do the right thing when popular opinion goes against them.

Social skills—from making introductions, to anger management, to using good manners—are wonderful, necessary tools. But let's not forget that they are precisely that—*tools,* not internalized virtues. *What's missing? Reflection.*

Source: Developed by Karen E. Bohlin, Center for the Advancement of Ethics and Character at Boston University.

Appendix O, "Developing a Yearlong Theme," outlines the high points of a plan for introducing a character education theme to a middle school classroom during the first day of school and then reinforcing it as the year progresses. The first week of school is a pivotal time. Students are particularly receptive to new approaches, and an effective teacher can set a positive and meaningful tone for the year. Before the year begins, consider carefully what theme, or message, you would like to emphasize and develop during the year. The theme illustrated in Appendix O, for example, is that our choices—especially how we choose to treat others—reveal our character.

Appendix P, "Elizabeth Barker, Prison Educator," is an example of using a particular reading, in this case a newspaper article, as a vehicle for discussing and reflecting on the importance of making good choices.

▶ Key Thoughts

The challenges that students face as they try to learn and to excel in school also present them with opportunities to develop and practice virtues that will enrich their lives.

▶ Discussion and Reflection Activities

To further come to grips with the importance of providing students with the opportunities to develop good character, complete these questions and activities:

- How can we help our students see learning in general as a moral responsibility and one that is enhanced by habits such as diligence, intellectual honesty, good judgment, courage, and persistence?

- Think back to an experience from childhood or adolescence that taught you something about perseverance, self-sacrifice, hard work, or kindness. Who was involved? Why did this virtue become meaningful or real to you?

- Think back to a particularly challenging class that you took when you were a student. What did you learn about yourself, and what virtues did you practice that have served you well later in life?

Chapter 5

Engaging Parents in Character Education

We strongly affirm parents as the primary moral educators of their children.

—THE CHARACTER EDUCATION MANIFESTO

The Tenth Commandment:
Thou Shalt Make Good Character a High Priority in Your Home
Parents and children have many pressures on them. They have many demands on their time and many distractions in their lives. The modern world is constantly screaming for our attention, time, and energies. Our children must know that our first concern for them is that they use their formative years to make themselves strong individuals, that they make themselves people of good character.

—KEVIN RYAN, "Building Character in Schools"

Do not protect your children from failure. Do not underestimate the value of getting caught. Some of the best lessons in life are learned through an in-house suspension or a visit to the police station.

—KAREN E. BOHLIN, "The Odyssey of Adolescence"

PARENTS ARE the primary moral educators of their children, and there are a number of things that schools can do to help them. This chapter looks at the importance of interaction among parents, teachers, and students on the subject of good character and also discusses the value of formal agreements between parents and schools.

Helping Parents Help Each Other

Some parents recently shared with the authors an experience that helped them when their relationship with their eighth-grade daughter was becoming increasingly unpleasant. Just when their patience had grown tissue thin, they received an unusual request from their daughter's teacher to attend a meeting for all of her students' parents. The ominous-sounding purpose of this meeting was to discuss "some problems that have developed recently."

This was only their daughter's second year at her school, so these parents had developed only casual relationships with the other parents. With no idea what "some problems" referred to, they were rather anxious about the meeting. So, too, it turned out, were the other parents. The teacher, a young woman still in her twenties, came right to the point. She was disturbed by the quality of the children's work and their lack of effort. She said that she did not have a solution, but she really felt the need to get the parents' insights and cooperation.

After a few defensive comments from the group, one father addressed a question to the other parents: "My Yvonne tells us that all the other kids in this class are allowed unlimited phone calls on school nights. Is that true?" That simple question opened a floodgate and was followed by a spirited discussion among the parents about the frequency, length, and inanity of their children's telephone calls.

Then the conversation turned to hanging out at the mall, and a similar pattern of anecdotes and complaints emerged. People started to relax and to laugh. Finally, the teacher, ignoring her own agenda, suggested that the parents list the topics of concern to them. Items such as sleepovers, exclusive parties, television watching, the Internet, makeup, language codes, allowances, the "in" group and the "out" group, and chores at home filled the blackboard. It was clearly too much to tackle in one night, so the parents decided to meet once a month until they ran out of steam. The last we heard, they were beginning their second year of monthly meetings. They had developed a clearer set of expectations and limitations for their adolescent children, and they had also begun planning weekend events and outings for the class.

The parents who told us this story reported that as a result of this experience, three things happened, besides the fact that their daughter began to talk with them more openly. First, they gained a great deal of confidence and nuggets of good advice from the other parents. Second, they became good friends with several of the other parents. Third, the teacher reported a dramatic change in the behavior of her class.

Parent groups and parent education programs are, slowly, growing in schools that have taken seriously the principle that parents are the primary moral educators of their children. In Northfield, Illinois, for instance, the Sunset Ridge School District initiated a parent education program two years ago by inviting parents to participate in a faculty in-service program on character development and teaching. The district then hosted a speaker to address the parents on character development and parenting. These events gave rise to a now very committed parent group, whose members meet monthly to read, discuss, and plan initiatives around character development in the home and to support one another as parents. Exhibit 5.1 offers an excerpt from the group's impressive quarterly newsletter.

The Montrose School in Natick, Massachusetts, a 1999 National School of Character, launched its parent education program by hosting speakers on parenting and character twice yearly for the community. The Parent Education Committee, with parents representing each grade level, dedicated

---

EXHIBIT 5.1

Excerpt from a Parent Group Newsletter

Tips on Choosing the Best Media Options for Your Children

The media has become such a powerful source in our lives and our children's lives that trying to decide what movies or TV shows to watch is quite complicated.

With all the videos, magazines, Internet sites, computer and Nintendo games to choose from, it can be confusing for adults as well as children.

"What is appropriate for my child?" is a question parents often ask. For each family, the answer will be different. While *Connections* doesn't have all the answers, we can help you determine what you want your child to watch by showing you where to get some guidelines.

What follows is a list of Internet sites that review movies.

http://www.screenlit.com

If you already have a movie, music or video in mind, this is the place to go for a summary. It includes reviews and tables that clearly pinpoint questionable content.

http://www.teachwithmovies.org

This is for older videos and movies. If you have a subject or virtue in mind, this lists movies by topic. The list is extensive. In print, there is a Family Video Guild (148 pages) for $8, and a semi-monthly Preview Family Movie and TV Review for $34/year. Contact PREVIEW, 1309 Seminole, Richardson, Texas 75080, phone (800) 807-8071, fax (972) 669-9040. (PREVIEW also has a website, www.previewonline.org with free mini-reviews.)

In our next issue, we'll review some movies, books, and websites for you. Any and all recommendations from parents are welcome!

In the meantime, some suggested movies include: *Air Bud 2, Golden Retriever*, rated PG; *Ever After*, rated PG-13; *I'll Be Home for Christmas*, rated PG; and *Life Is Beautiful*, rated PG-13.

Source: Character Education Connections, Dec. 2000.

a large portion of its time to the development of the *Parents' Guide,* a booklet designed to help parents understand the school's commitment to academic and character excellence and to show them how they can work more effectively with the school to help their children achieve these twin goals. The booklet covers a number of topics. Here is a sampling from the table of contents: "The Montrose Approach," "Character Development," "Academic Excellence," "Parents and Teachers Collaboration," "Continuing Education Programs for Parents," "The Montrose Graduate," "Parents on Parenthood," "Home and School Partnership."

Although a school can often spearhead a parent education initiative, it is recommended that parent groups be created and sustained by the parents themselves and that the priority stay firmly on educating and supporting parents. The school can be most helpful by supplying a forum for meeting and by providing channels of communication among all the parents in the school community.

▶ Key Thoughts

Because parents are the primary moral educators of their children, schools undertaking character education should build a partnership with the home. One thing that schools can do is to bring parents together and give them a forum for constructive dialogue.

▶ Discussion and Reflection Activities

To begin improving school support for parents, discuss staff responses to these questions:

- How would you describe your school's working relationship with students' parents? Does it feel cooperative or adversarial? What can be done to improve or strengthen this relationship?

- What is the school already doing to communicate with parents? Where could it improve?

- What is the school already doing to help parents interact with one another? What more could it do?

▶ Best Practice Stories

Parents at Emperor Elementary School in San Gabriel, California, are considered to be the students' primary teachers and therefore necessary school partners. Each year the parents are asked to enter into a home and school *compact.* This compact asks them to commit to working together with the school in the education of their children, "our shared students." Parents also hear about character education lessons, events, and ideas in the weekly teacher newsletter, which also includes ideas for home-based activities. The school also sends home a copy of the Eagle "I's"—the school's code of conduct—to post on the refrigerator. "One of our moms said that a couple of summers ago she wasn't getting anywhere with enforcing her expectations," says Principal Kathy Perini. "She dragged her son over to the fridge, pointed to the Eagle "I's" and said, 'This is how we are operating this summer.' It worked, because it was a language he understood."

Cotswold Elementary School in Charlotte, North Carolina, hosted Parent to Parent, a lecture series focusing on good parenting. During the ten sessions, parents were paired with other parents. "One of the best things about Parent to Parent was that parents got to see that they all had the same concerns about their kids. They realized that they all wanted the same things for their kindergarten students. It brought us together," said Mrs. Henry, one of Cotswold's teachers.

Promoting Parent-Child Interaction

Schools that promote character also promote parent-child interaction. The Hazelwood School in Louisville, Kentucky, for example, has turned the traditional science fair competition on its head. Instead of assigning projects that students and some parents sink exorbitant time and money into (eagerly expecting an award), the school asks students to invite their parents to an annual schoolwide event where parents and students work together on science experiments. Parents and their children learn together, and many parents have remarked that the evening affords them the opportunity to spend quality time with their children in a way not ordinarily possible.

There are numerous possibilities for similar initiatives. For example, schools have sponsored craft fairs where parents and children come not to purchase crafts but to learn together how to make a craft item. Brookside Elementary, a 1998 National School of Character, has hosted Shut-Off the TV Night, inviting families to come to the school instead for an evening of games and events. Increasingly, parents are being called upon to serve as guest speakers in classrooms, sharing their professional expertise, talents, and hobbies and offering insights about the good habits or the virtue needed to exercise these talents well. What we see in all of these examples are schools and families joining forces to foster a spirited community of learning and virtue.

▶ Key Thoughts

Going to school can change children and sometimes pull them away from their parents' world of ideas, interests, and values. Well-planned activities can foster parent-child interaction and reinforce your school's core virtues.

▶ Discussion and Reflection Activity

Begin developing special opportunities for parents to interact with their children by brainstorming answers to this question:

- What activities can your school plan to bring students together with their parents?

▶ Best Practice Story

At Columbine Elementary School in Woodland Park, Colorado, the school library is particularly animated, featuring student projects, books, and murals. A parent recalls discovering a group of fourth-graders in one room who were reading and discussing biographies. "When I asked them about the colorful backpacks lined up along the walls, they explained that they were family backpacks. Families were welcome to check a backpack out from the library and enjoy a set of engaging learning activities together. The backpacks were designed thematically—focusing on explorers or dinosaurs, for example—and included games, videos, read-aloud books, and so on. The children and Columbine families said they loved borrowing these 'Family Packs.'"

Drawing Up Parent Agreements

At Hyde School, a nationally recognized private boarding school in Bath, Maine, character development is fundamentally a family affair. "We do not take kids unless parents make a commitment to go through our character development program," says Joseph W. Gauld, the school's founder. In this program, parents gather monthly for parent meetings, retreats, and family weekends. They are asked to look within themselves, find their strengths and weaknesses, and strive to better themselves, for their own sake as well as for their child's sake. "You have to start with the principle that parents are the primary teachers and home is the primary classroom. . . . If you get to the parents, you get to the kids," says Gauld.

Some schools ask parents to sign contracts spelling out what they will do to foster their children's education. But sometimes the word *contract* has a legalistic connotation that schools and families would prefer not to emphasize. So, instead, they draw up *agreements*, *covenants*, or even *promises* to support their children and the school. To be effective these agreements should generally include a delineation of the academic and character expectations the school holds for its students. Additional expectations will vary based on the needs of the students and families in different communities. For example, one school may ask that parents provide their children with breakfast and school supplies, whereas another school may see this as an unfair demand. School leaders and teachers must exercise good judgment when drawing up such documents, seeing them as a positive agreement between the school and the family to serve students better rather than simply as leverage for holding parents or teachers more accountable for what they fail to do.

▶ Key Thoughts

Parents are schools' and teachers' most important allies in making the school a community of virtue. Consider drawing up an agreement that will help your students' parents understand how they can work with the school to achieve this end.

▶ Discussion and Reflection Activity

Consider what your students need from their parents to be better learners as you answer this question:

- What could parents do to help you improve the moral and educational environment at your school?

▶ Best Practice Story

At Newsome Park Elementary School in Newport News, Virginia, all parents sign the "Parent, Student, Teacher Contract," which outlines the responsibilities of each of these three segments of the school community. The contract is one of the cornerstones of the school's character education program.

The parents' portion of the contract asks them to provide a home environment that will encourage and stimulate learning by discussing schoolwork with their children; modeling the importance of learning; and fostering a positive respect for school, curriculum, teachers, and staff.

In their portion the students agree to take responsibility for fulfilling all class work and homework assignments; to attend school regularly and promptly; to follow rules and regulations, including the dress code; and to demonstrate respect for authority, property, and the rights of others.

Teachers affirm their commitment to emphasizing basic academic skills, community service learning, and character education; providing a positive, safe, and orderly environment; regularly notifying parents of students' academic progress and conduct; and using technology to enhance instruction.

Keeping in Touch with Parents

Word that a school is embarking on a character education program often provokes a mixed response in a community. Although many parents, trustful and supportive of the school, will immediately rally behind the effort, others will be wary. Some will bring up such objections as, "Aren't they having enough trouble teaching the regular subjects? Why are they getting into this area?" or, "My daughter has her family and her church to help her with her character. Why is the school getting so involved?" or, "Who are these teachers to start preaching virtue and goodness? Stick to the basics!"

It is vitally important, therefore, that educators stay in close communication with parents about the scope and content of character education efforts. Here are a few ideas for keeping in touch:

- Hold orientation meetings that include open discussion about the school's core virtues and how they should be integrated into the school's policies and curriculum. (Ideally, parents will have participated in selecting the core virtues, as discussed in Chapter Two.)

- Invite a guest speaker to one of these meetings to talk about building healthy relationships with adolescents or parenting and character development.

- Send out a parent newsletter to keep parents aware of what is currently being done to promote character in the school. This newsletter could be used as well to seek parents' help in dealing with schoolwide problems, such as verbal put-downs or other forms of cruelty and exclusion.

- Send a monthly message from the school principal to parents, each message discussing one of the school's core virtues.

▶ Key Thoughts

Your school should communicate with parents early and often. There are many ways to do this, including orientation meetings, guest speakers, newsletters, and regular messages from the principal.

▶ Discussion and Reflection Activity

To focus your communications effectively, answer this question (or use it as the focus of a brainstorming activity):

- What two or three methods of communication would be most effective with the parents in your community?

▶ Best Practice Story

At the Benjamin Franklin Classical Charter School, a monthly newsletter not only updates parents on the *umbrella virtue* for the month but also offers

"With the challenges of today's society, parents are often left feeling as though they have no control over their children's influences. Although I will never be able to shield my children from the 'evils' of the world, I have peace of mind knowing that when they go to school at Atlantis each day, they are being instructed in the ways of kindness, compassion, and caring. I am very proud to say that my child goes to Atlantis Elementary where character truly counts."

—PARENT, Atlantis Elementary School, Cocoa, Florida

narrative snippets about the curricular and community service activities through which students are coming to understand and practice that and other virtues. It also includes *family service* and *family reading* suggestions, to give parents creative ideas for reinforcing the virtues at home. Additionally, each month each teacher sends home a *scope and sequence* page covering what will be taught in the upcoming month. This page is a preview of the reading, history, science, and math activities that the teacher has planned. Parents are encouraged to use this information and to support and supplement their child's learning at home.

Promoting Moral Conversations Between Parents and Children

Both parents and family psychologists acknowledge that maintaining contact with children gets more and more difficult once they leave the early grades. But the understanding that comes with ongoing communication and trust is essential to being a good parent.

Schools can be very helpful in initiating and deepening the exchanges between parents and their children. For example, the Loving Well Project, a literature-based curriculum created for middle school students, introduces children to the moral issues surrounding romance, love, and sexuality. The curriculum includes many homework assignments, but among the most popular are the ones that ask young adolescents to interview their parents on such topics as their first kiss and when they first felt they were in love. Although on the face of it such a conversation is not necessarily a moral lesson, it certainly provides a platform for parents to begin discussing a major moral topic.

This is just one example of a curriculum topic related to character education. History and English lessons are filled with topics and themes that can foster conversations about values and virtues. English teachers can ask students to discuss with their parents the person who has had the most positive impact on the parents' lives, to write a short essay on a parent's hero and state why the parent thinks the individual is heroic, or to talk to a parent about the biggest obstacle the parent has overcome and what helped him or her overcome it. Social studies teachers might have students interview their parents about the individual the parents think was the most influential person of the twentieth century, or talk to their parents about what could be done to improve race relations in the community and then write a short paper on the parents' ideas. Besides drawing parents closer to what is going on in the school, such assignments give parents and students practice in having real conversations about their moral principles, what they believe is important in life, and (frequently a topic of great interest to teenagers) what Mom and Dad were like when they were young.

For younger students, consider sending home occasional *parent-child homework*—a fun, educational assignment that requires parent and child to work together.

The newsletter article in Exhibit 5.2 is an example of reaching out to parents on the subject of having moral conversations with their children; it makes parents aware of a specific problem and gives them tools they can use at home to help their own children change certain behaviors.

▶ Key Thoughts

Schools can do many things to help initiate meaningful conversations between students and their parents, their primary moral educators.

▶ Discussion and Reflection Activities

Good intergenerational conversations usually don't just happen. Teachers give students both the competence and confidence to conduct meaningful oral histories by helping them develop good questions and questioning skills. A well-structured assignment will also provide students with a focus for their conversation.

- Discuss specific assignments students could be given that would promote reflective discourse with their parents or other adults. (For example, students might interview a parent or grandparent about recollections of military service during a war or the Great Depression or more simply about how they used their time, enjoyed themselves, or supported their families when they were younger.)

- Consider the best ways to structure these assignments. (For example, students might begin this assignment by devising an interview questionnaire that invites conversation about personal qualities and memorable formative experiences, especially those relating to understanding a particular virtue.)

EXHIBIT 5.2

Example of a Newsletter Article That Promotes Moral Conversations

ON THE HOMEFRONT

The Full Circle Family Foundation

Parent's Topic: TEASING

Teasing can take different forms. It can range from attention-grabbing behavior to more serious harassment and bullying. It can be limited to sibling teasing or can extend to school and other social settings. Your child may be the target of teasing or be the one who teases—perhaps sometimes one, then the other. Teasing is an excellent touchpoint for focusing on the development of *respect, empathy,* and *courage* in your children.

Understanding RESPECT

Respect is the attitude and actions by which a person shows that s/he values another person. It is the practice of giving one's attention to another person, considering another worthy of high regard or esteem.

Respect in Action

Think about the reasons for teasing in your family. Three common reasons include a child's:

- Desire to get what he wants—being "one-up" on siblings or playmates
- Frustration with another child's lack of ability
- Attention-seeking behavior

Often the cause may be that one child isn't getting what he wants so he "takes it out" on the other. Helping your child to understand and accept the word "no" can help him to respect the right of the person who said it.

Encourage older children to be patient with younger ones—not to tease while playing a game, for example. Role-playing can help them understand the harm that too much teasing can do and can lead them to respect the feelings of a younger sibling. Try asking, "how do you feel when Sam makes fun of you at baseball? Well that's how Suzie feels when you tease her about her dolls."

Sometimes teasing just happens when there is "nothing better to do." Teasing can be a good way to get attention and often negative attention can seem better than no attention at all.

Family Respect Checklist

- How do we show that we care about each other's feelings?
- Is everyone treated as equally important in the family?
- Do we listen to one another without interruption?
- Do we listen politely to each other's stories and ideas? Or are they dismissed casually, laughed at, or criticized?
- Do we avoid put-downs in our family?
- Do we protect playmates at our house from teasing from others? *"In our house, we do not make fun of each other."*

Understanding EMPATHY

Empathy is the ability to recognize and identify with the feelings or thoughts of another person—to sense what another person is feeling and to imagine what it must be like. While the seeds of empathy may be natural in children, they need to be developed and nurtured.

Empathy in Action

Empathy is a virtue that children must learn through practice and help from their parents. Listening to others and reading body language are two practical ways that children can begin to understand how to empathize with others. This virtue is fostered in two ways:

- Help the child recognize the actions and the facial expressions that give clues to the feelings of others. Can they recognize the signals that their teasing has gone too far? These signals might be the other child becoming angry, quiet or withdrawn. Your child needs to recognize these signals and know when teasing has gone too far.
- Once the feelings have been recognized, encourage your child to identify with those feelings. Help him or her imagine how the other person might feel. You can teach this aspect of empathy by reminding your child of how s/he felt the last time he was teased by friends or classmates.

When children have gone too far in their teasing, focusing attention on the hurt that their behavior caused the other child can help them begin to empathize. Instead of "why did you do that? That was mean!"—try "how do you think Laura felt when you did that?"

Family Empathy Checklist

- How forgiving are the members of your family? How forgiving are you of yourself?
- Do you have unrealistic expectations of yourself? Of your spouse? Of your kids?
- Are you always hurried, more focused on activities than people?
- Are your reactions to accidents in proportion to their importance? (Think of the spilled milk!)
- Is it OK to talk about our feelings in our family? Do we talk about others' feelings?

Understanding COURAGE

Courage is the ability to recognize and refrain from a negative action such as teasing. Courage means doing the right thing, speaking out on behalf of others when necessary. It takes courage to stand up and "call others off" from teasing. It takes courage and strength of character to "bite your tongue" at your first reaction. It takes courage to apologize for something that hurt another person.

Courage in Action

You can foster courage in your child as he faces the problem of teasing by helping him to:
- Recognize when to refrain and to stand up to peer pressure.
- Recognize that when he is uncomfortable with teasing, the situation has probably gone too far, and then he needs to have the courage to resist it.
- Create boundaries by saying that "in our house, teasing is not allowed."
- Discover what he has in common with peers—they are less likely to tease someone they have gotten to know.

Family Courage Checklist

- Do we own up to mistakes in our family?
- Do we apologize when we have hurt or offended someone else?

- Do we talk about examples of courage in everyday life?
- Can we disagree in our house without being criticized?
- Do we support each other when someone has "gone out on a limb" and shown courage?

With common sense, back-to-basics suggestions from experienced parents and the practical advice of scholars, teachers, and experts in character education, Full Circle strives to offer parents accessible approaches for thinking through the realities of raising their children with a focus on developing virtue.

Source: The Full Circle Family Foundation, reprinted in *Character* (newsletter of the Center for the Advancement of Ethics and Character), Summer 2001.

Chapter 6

The Teacher's Work
Nurturing Character

> Each of us must come to care about everyone else's children.
> We must recognize that the welfare of our children is intimate-
> ly linked to the welfare of all other people's children. After all,
> when one of our children needs life-saving surgery, someone
> else's child will perform it. If one of our children is harmed by
> violence, someone else's child will be responsible for the vio-
> lent act. The good life for our own children can be secured only
> if a good life is also secured for all other people's children.
>
> —LILIAN KATZ

> I touch the future. I teach.
>
> —CHRISTA MCAULIFFE, motto

EDUCATING FOR VIRTUE is about awakening students' minds and hearts to new possibilities and pointing them in the right direction. This chapter focuses on the many things teachers can do to carry out this task both in the classroom and in the school as a whole.

Six Ways to Promote Good Character

Six words—the six E's—describe how educators can promote moral development within each student, the classroom, and the entire school environment:

Example

As teachers, we are always on exhibit, always being studied by our students. They often know our limited wardrobe better than we do. They notice when we've gotten a haircut or when we're long overdue for one. But they are perhaps most skilled at discerning who we are. They draw their conclusions from the way we habitually treat students and colleagues, the way we prepare and lead our classes, the way we deal with disappointment, mistakes, and humiliation. Ultimately, it is the *person,* not the teacher, who makes a lasting impression on his or her students.

Take time to reflect on your professional habits and relationships with others at your school. Do these reflect the virtues that you hope to inspire in your students?

Explanation

To enhance our students' understanding of specific virtues, we need to offer explanations. The more contextualized we can make virtue, the better. For example, a fourth-grade class might observe what the virtue of respect looks like on a field trip to the theater, noting everything from the atmosphere on the bus to the applause at the theater to people's behavior at lunch at McDonald's. The more we grow accustomed to using and explaining the language of virtue, the more children will understand what words like *patience, consideration,* and *integrity* really mean.

Consider your school's core virtues. Do you take time to point out and explain these virtues in the context of your students' lives and daily activities?

Ethos, or the Ethical Environment

As we discussed earlier, classrooms and schools are ethical communities, either good or bad. Teachers play a key part in cultivating and sustaining the ethos of these communities. As educators, we have to help our students see that civility, courtesy, and friendship matter. We cannot simply invoke rules to gain commitment from students. We need to foster relationships based on trust and mutual respect.

Does your school's ethos reflect its core virtues? Are ethical questions—such as what's the right thing to do?—part of the classroom dialogue?

Experience

Experience is one of our greatest teachers, and many virtues—such as *perseverance, consideration,* and *responsibility*—can be cultivated simply by doing one's work well. Virtues also arise from struggling against negative peer pressure or being willing to learn from one' mistakes, failures, and disappointments. But for such experience to be instructive, teachers need to help students make sense of it. For example, they need to invite students to reflect on their visit to a children's hospital; they need to prompt students to think about what they can learn from a particularly low test score or from not getting a callback for the school play.

Are you and others at your school helping students to gain the most from their positive and negative experiences?

Exhortation

Character education is achieved not only by example and explanation but also by inspiration. Someone once said, "A mediocre teacher tells, a good teacher explains, a superior teacher demonstrates, but the great teacher inspires." We should not underestimate the power of inspiration and hope in the face of discouragement or the power of admonishment in the face of intolerable behavior such as cruel teasing and cheating. Students need to know that we care about the kind of people they are becoming.

Do educators at your school use occasional exhortation to remind students of the proper course of action or to lift them out of the dumps?

Expectations of Excellence

A 1998 study by the Public Agenda Foundation revealed that "three-fourths of teens enjoy going to school, but most have serious complaints about the atmosphere and quality of education. Half the students surveyed say their school does not challenge them to do their best; two-thirds feel they're not living up to their potential; and three-fourths believe they would learn more if there were higher standards."[1] That's the bad news. The good news is that students can do more, and they want to be challenged. Our task as educators is to tap their potential.

Do educators at your school believe in the potential of their students, and are students at your school challenged?

▶ Key Thoughts

Virtue is at the heart of teaching and learning. As educators of the minds and characters of young people, teachers have a profound impact not only on individual performance but also on the kinds of persons that their students are becoming.

▶ Discussion and Reflection Activities

Think back on all the teachers you have had since kindergarten, and then complete these questions and activities:

- Which teacher had an impact on your character, on the person you have become?

- How did he or she make that impression? What was it about him or her that you found inspiring, admirable, or worthy of emulation?

- Commit one of these ideas to writing and then set a practical goal for your own personal and professional development. Share this goal with those doing these activities with you, listen to their goals, and arrange to support each other in achieving these goals. Alternatively, share this goal with another colleague or mentor, and periodically check with this other person informally for encouragement and support.

▶ Best Practice Story

Melissa was not the child Mrs. Parken worried about. She performed above grade level in every subject and was enthusiastic about school. She played jump rope with the girls and basketball with the boys, and her mom was the room mother. The sixth-grader that Mrs. Parken worried about was Lucia. Lucia was a new student, in a neighborhood school that received only a handful of new students each year. Large for her age anyway, Lucia had hit puberty early. Her clothes didn't quite fit (or quite match), and her hair was never quite combed. If Lucia were quiet, the students could have quietly ignored her. But she wasn't. She had an opinion on everything and everybody, and she had a habit of jumping into conversations even when the other girls sent clear signals that she was not welcome. Soon the teasing began, from playground taunts to guarded classroom snickers whenever she made a comment. Melissa never snickered, but she did send a few knowing smiles; she never teased, but she said nothing when other students did; and when Lucia approached a group of chatting girls, Melissa corroborated their silent message: "You are not welcome here."

Two months into the school year, Mrs. Parken asked Melissa to stay after school for a few minutes. "I want to tell you something I haven't told the other students," she said. "Lucia's parents were divorced recently. She had to leave her old school and her old friends to come here. She could use a friend right now. I thought you should know." Later that night, Melissa started to cry as she related the story to her mother. "I know I should be her friend. . . . But I don't really like her." "Have you given her a chance to be liked?" replied her mother.

Melissa didn't sleep well that night. She did not befriend Lucia the next day—but she began to watch her more carefully. She watched how Lucia sat alone and bit her lip nervously before coming to "join" a conversation. She noticed how Lucia's shoulders tensed when the boys giggled at her during class. When Melissa noticed that Lucia knew a lot about taking care of animals—a subject that interested Melissa as well—she asked Mrs. Parken after class if they could be assigned as project partners. The teacher nodded thoughtfully: "We could do that."

Building Commitment to Character Education at Your School

Philip Tate, a professor of education at Boston University, has done research on excellence in teaching and the characteristics that distinguish teachers as excellent. From a study of over a thousand teachers who have been nominated as teachers of the year (representing a range of grade levels and subjects), he offers three main findings:[2]

1. An excellent teacher serves as a counselor or adviser to students.

2. An excellent teacher stimulates and motivates, awakening students' interest in learning.

3. An excellent teacher is committed and dedicated; such teachers "show interest in their students, their school, their teaching, and their field."

Each of these traits speaks more about teachers as people and about their relationships with their students than about their knowledge base or skills. These traits define teachers who throw themselves into their work with students. And these traits are reflected in the seven competencies the authors believe essential for character educators, listed in Exhibit 6.1.

Four Virtues

The characteristics Tate has identified rest mainly on four specific virtues, discussed in the following paragraphs. Cultivating these virtues within themselves can help teachers make the commitment to character education.

Professional Responsibility

Being committed to character education does not mean becoming a moral missionary, preaching to students about goodness at every turn. Concern for the moral life of students must be balanced, free of excessive didacticism and tedious moralizing. At a more fundamental level, teachers must show their commitment by regular performance of their professional responsibilities, including starting classes on time, being well prepared to teach, correcting papers promptly, being a supportive colleague, and being available to students who are in trouble or in need, whether it be academic or personal.

Trust

As public school teachers, staff, and administrators, we have an enormous obligation to preserve the public trust placed in us by parents, students, and community members. At the same time, we need to show our students that we trust them. Students come to school with myriad fears, from fear of

---

EXHIBIT 6.1

The Seven Competencies of Character Educators

1. Teachers must be able to exemplify good character and character building themselves. They need not be paragons of virtue, but they must be visibly *at work* on their own character.
2. Teachers must be able to make the development of their students' moral life and character a professional responsibility and a priority.
3. Teachers must be able to engage students in moral discourse about the *oughtness* of life; they must be able to talk to students about what is right and what is wrong in life.
4. Teachers must be able to articulate clearly their own position on a range of ethical issues, yet not unnecessarily burden students with personal views and opinions.
5. Teachers must be able to help children empathize with the experience of others—helping them get outside themselves and into the world of others.
6. Teachers must be able to establish in their classrooms a positive moral ethos, an environment characterized by high ethical standards and respect for all.
7. Teachers must be able to provide activities, in the school and in the community, that give students experience and practice in behaving ethically and altruistically. In effect, they must help their students become moral actors.

---

being bullied to fear of not living up to Mom's or Dad's expectations. They need to know that the adults in the school trust them and believe in them, sharing the conviction that we can all learn from our mistakes and even our failures. Trust, as leadership experts contend, is one of the most powerful human motivators.

Moral Courage

Young people need to see moral courage before they can put it into practice. Children and adolescents look first to adults to see how we live by our convictions, to understand why we tolerate some things and put our foot down on others. They need to lean on the courage of adults until they develop their own. They rely on adults to intervene swiftly and decisively when learning, individual dignity, or physical safety is at stake.

Justice

Along with responsibility, trust, and moral courage, we also need to practice the virtue of justice. Children recognize justice (and its counterpart, injustice) from a very young age. They begin the "that's not fair" cry as early as three years of age. Justice is not a matter of treating everybody the same; rather it is about giving each student what he or she needs. It's a matter of being sensitive to the circumstances of our individual students, taking time to do what's right, and being respectful of their dignity and potential.

And the Little Things

In a virtuous community even the little things express the good character of the people. Chapter Three discusses building a community of virtue for students by, among other methods, attending to the little things that make life more pleasant for students. This can boost morale in a few short months. Here are some of the little things teachers and staff have identified as being important ways for teachers and staff to show respect for one another:

- Notifying someone immediately when the photocopier jams.
- Not letting the paper or ink run low in the copy machine
- Keeping the coffeepot clean and washing up after using dishes
- Identifying creative themes and topics for lunch conversations (favorite films, books, good jokes or games, for example) in place of gossiping or complaining about students and the administration
- Putting things back where they belong after borrowing them
- Keeping the faculty room orderly and cheerful; applying a clean coat of paint when necessary
- Surprising colleagues with inspirational quotes or poems, doing small favors such as taking someone's class when he or she needs a mental health break
- Celebrating birthdays
- Eliminating swearing

▶ **Key Thoughts**

As it says in *The Character Education Manifesto*, "the teacher and the school principal are central to this enterprise [of character education] and must be educated, selected, and encouraged with this mission in mind. In truth, all of the adults in the school must embody and reflect the moral authority which has been invested in them by the parents and the community."

▶ **Discussion and Reflection Activities**

In the following activity of identifying your own little things, remember to be professional, practical, and constructive with your suggestions.

- Reflect on some pet-peeves or annoyances that come up in the course of the school day (for example, the copier is always out of paper, the teachers' work room is left messy, and the like). What can be done to reduce or eliminate these annoyances? Discuss your ideas with colleagues and prioritize one to three realistic goals that you can commit to in an effort to improve the working environment.

▶ **Best Practice Story**

Ten teachers from Longfellow Elementary School in Hastings, Nebraska, sacrificed time in the middle of the year to invest in the development of character education in their school. They traveled ninety minutes each way to take a semester-long course titled "Ethics in Education" at the University of Nebraska at Lincoln. In the following semester they took an independent study course in which they assessed schoolwide character education initiatives.

Feeding the Teachers So They Don't Eat the Children

Teachers and administrators need intellectual stimulation and inspiration as much if not more than students do. They need time to make sense of and shape the character education philosophy and core virtues of the school. They need to understand this effort in terms of their own lives and in terms of their work with students. In the authors' experience, educators and school employees need time away from routine daily demands to partake of one another's experience and wisdom.

There are a variety of ways to foster reflection among faculty and staff. For example, some schools provide inspirational quotations and incisive readings on character for all school employees, perhaps by way of a monthly newsletter or message. Other schools have initiated voluntary reading groups on the subject of character for teachers and staff. This activity can be organized as an optional block during scheduled in-service time, as a segment of regular faculty meetings, or as a voluntary after-school activity.

The common fruit of such initiatives is that teachers feel energized by the shared study and inquiry with their colleagues. Having a common text—whether it is an article, poem, chapter, or book—gives them some distance from the daily grind and frees them to think about questions related to ethics and character in a fresh context. They find that through their discussions they are able to offer support and suggestions to one another about teaching, developing curriculum, and being effective with students. Finally, many educators "fill their well" with inspiring and nourishing ideas by attending institutes and teacher conferences. (Appendix B lists a number of works relevant to character education and thus to teachers who are working to develop virtues in their own lives and in the lives of their students.)

▶ **Key Thoughts**

Cultivating the intellectual lives of teachers and rejuvenating their sense of commitment to teaching should be a priority. Teachers are constantly giving of themselves—their time, energy, and intellectual resources—to their students. We need to afford them the time and space to refuel, to cultivate their intellectual lives, and to nurture that calling that drew many of them into teaching in the first place. They also need to be able to take the time to recognize each other's professional contributions, to offer moral support, and to boost each other's morale.

▶ Discussion and Reflection Activities

Challenging encounters with science, literature, and history and a forum for reading, writing, and discussion, offer teachers both an intellectual stretch and opportunity to renew their enthusiasm for learning. Consider the following questions and complete the activity to begin preparing such encounters and defining this forum:

- What opportunities can we build into our ongoing faculty meetings and committee work to foster more reflection and dialogue?

- In what setting can we begin to discuss, formally or informally, inspirational books (one chapter at a time) in order to promote collegiality and professional esteem?

- How can we enrich professional development and study opportunities for our teachers and staff?

- Set one goal for reading or writing about the dignity of teaching and the development of character through teaching.

▶ Best Practice Stories

At Pattonville High School in Maryland Heights, Missouri, during their monthly, hourlong staff development block, teachers gather for optional workshops. A reading group that took up William Bennett's *The Book of Virtues* last year and began his sequel, *The Moral Compass*, in 1998 has won the faithful attendance of nearly one-third of the faculty. "We don't limit our discussion to school," social studies chair Leonard Sullivan says. "Often we talk about our personal lives and family experiences."

After reading the chapter in *The Book of Virtues* titled "Hearth and Home," members of the group discussed how they could help students from broken homes. As a consequence of participating in the reading group, one teacher also reported being "able to use one of the stories to help a student who was having a really difficult time." Another teacher opted to address Aristotle's definition of true friendship in his unit on Greece. In short, what these teachers contend is that time spent in guided reflection and study has a tremendous payback.

The faculty at Hilltop Elementary School in Lynnwood, Washington, knew that proactively searching for and implementing new ideas was essential to the success of their character education program. They added resource books to the school library, viewed videos together (such as Barbara Coloroso's *Winning at Teaching Without Beating Your Kids*), and traveled to Thomas Lickona's summer institute on character education in Cortland, New York. Every year, Hilltop hosts its own Character Education Conference, bringing in nationally renowned presenters. The purpose of these conferences is twofold, says Principal Geri Branch: validation and promotion. "[First] we want to provide a full afternoon of celebration for Hilltop staff for what they do. It's a valuing of their work. Our second goal is outreach. We invite all of our district to attend and even some beyond our district."

Chapter 7

Helping Students Take Command

> The young do not know enough to be prudent, and therefore
> they attempt the impossible—and achieve it generation after
> generation.
>
> —PEARL S. BUCK

CHARACTER FORMATION is an individual process. Some children respond
to the call early on and with great intensity. Others aggressively resist our
efforts to help them. Some are challenged to shape their character by a life
they encounter in a book. Others respond to an athletic coach's prodding.
Still others are moved to change by working with the less fortunate. There
is no one sure road to acquiring a strong moral character. This chapter looks
at the many factors we need to consider as we help students internalize virtue. We need to raise their awareness of what it takes to develop good character, inspire their understanding and desire to live virtuously, and give
them opportunities to practice virtue and reflect on their choices. In short,
this chapter focuses on ways of helping students internalize good habits of
mind, heart, and action.

Responding to Different Ages and Stages

In addition to varying from individual to individual, the process of character formation varies greatly from age to age and stage to stage. Thus the par-
ticulars of what a classroom teacher does with her students will depend
very much on what grade level she teaches. The character education challenge for a kindergarten teacher might be to get her new students to stop
running around the classroom, whereas a high school science teacher might

be trying to encourage his seniors to develop greater respect for lab science and the importance of not falsifying data.

Child psychologist and educator David Isaacs points out that specific virtues are best cultivated at particular developmental stages.[1] He stresses, for instance, that children age seven and younger do not have the necessary knowledge or experience to rely on their own judgment or authority; they need to trust and listen to the adults who care for them. Hence, for this age group, the virtue of obedience is essential. Order is another important virtue to instill in the youngster, so that he learns how to take care of his toys and clothes, putting them back where they belong and contributing to the overall care of the home or classroom. Generosity, too, needs to be taught quite explicitly at this age.

Isaacs suggests that between the ages of seven and twelve, when children's will begins to assert itself more, virtues such as diligence and courage can strengthen children's character and help them channel their energies and desires properly instead of impulsively. Then, as their reasoning powers mature in adolescence, the virtues of understanding, practical wisdom, and good judgment should be cultivated more deliberately. This developmental scheme offers a helpful framework for implementing character education. Although at all three stages, habits of the mind, heart, and action should be engaged, it is clear that there are age-appropriate emphases.

▶ Key Thoughts

Different ages and stages of development call for different approaches in character education. In the earlier years greater emphasis should be placed on properly guiding action toward good habits and practices—from sharing playthings to hanging up one's coat. In the middle years the mind and the heart become the locus of character education.

Some schools are formally applying this kind of knowledge about children's moral development to their character education efforts. Appendix H, "Rubrics for Students," for example, contains the seven Personal and Social Responsibility Standards that are applied at Columbine Elementary School and displays the chart the school has drawn up to show what these standards mean at each grade level. Use this appendix to inspire your school community as it develops its own rubrics for students.

▶ Discussion and Reflection Activities

To help students see virtue in action, use these activities to begin developing age-appropriate operational definitions of core virtues. (Operational definitions are behaviorally specific.)

- List your school's core virtues and definitions. Then divide into groups by grade level. Create a grid defining what one (or two or more) of these core virtues looks like in the classroom, on the playground, and on the school bus. (This activity can be conducted quite successfully with students as well. Students are quite articulate about what fairness and respect look like. The challenge is to keep them reflective and accountable for their own choices and actions. Are they behaving in ways consistent with what they have helped to define as respectful, kind, diligent, and so forth?)

- If you wish, take this activity further by creating a rubric like Columbine Elementary's or by inviting students to reflect on their progress in living the core virtues each term.

- Discuss how well your school links behaviors and skills—from responsibility for completing homework well to welcoming new students to the school—to virtue in order to help students internalize good habits. When students think teachers are interested only in prescribed behaviors or skills, they will learn to perform. When they know teachers are more interested in the ideal that motivates behavior—for example, responsibility for learning and respect for all persons—students are more likely to want to make these habits and skills their own.

▶ Best Practice Story

To facilitate virtuous behavior, one teacher uses a list of ways to join in a discussion that reminds students what respect looks like and sounds like during class meetings:

"I agree (disagree) because . . ."

"I'm unclear about . . ."

"I'd like to add to _____'s points . . ."

"I'm confused about . . ."

NO PUT-DOWNS

Another teacher displays these reminders to help students make ethical decisions:

Before you make a choice, ask yourself . . .

"What does my conscience say about it?"

"Could it hurt anyone, including me?"

"Is it fair?"

"Would it violate the Golden Rule?"

"Have I ever been told it's wrong?"

"Deep down, how do I feel about this decision?"

Giving Your Students What They Really Need

In the end, each child is responsible for developing his or her own character. As it says in *The Character Education Manifesto*, "young people need to realize that forging their own characters is an essential and demanding life task. And the sum of their school experiences—in successes and failures, both academic and athletic, both intellectual and social—provides much of the raw material for this personal undertaking." This resource book is full of practical ideas that educators can use to help young people become interested in and assume ownership for this essential, lifetime task. Here are a few more:

Take Time to Listen to Your Students

To begin with, decide to become a better listener. Over and over again, children and adolescents report that no one listens to them and no one understands them. They have questions, uncertainties, and huge insecurities, and the adult world all too often turns a deaf ear to them. Listening to your students and listening well, by making eye contact and giving your full attention, sends a powerful message to them. When students are taken seriously by others, they begin to take themselves seriously.

Careful listening lets students know that we take them seriously. It communicates that we have true regard for them and that they are worth our time and attention.

Inspire Your Students by Seeing Them for Who They Can Be

Having been fed a constant diet of scandals, flawed heroes, and human deceit, our media-saturated students are frequently quite suspicious of life. Despite this cynicism, young people hunger for ideals and heroes to guide their lives. Teachers who are able to motivate students, to inspire them to go well beyond what they thought was possible, have two important qualities. First, they allow students to see that the teacher is on their side, rooting for them. Second, they are able to communicate trust; for example, they might give a troubled student the responsibility for collecting the money for a field trip. These teachers communicate trust without threats or conditions. They offer trust with the confidence that students will do well what is expected of them. Although teachers have to be ready to tolerate failures and pick up the pieces, this kind of trust from them brings out the best in many students.

Teachers who inspire their students see the best in them and are willing to take a chance by trusting in students' best efforts.

Decide to Love Your Students

Human beings crave love, and much of the trouble students get into—from disrupting classrooms to promiscuous sexual behavior—comes down to, as the song goes, "lookin' for love in all the wrong places."

Some scholars make a distinction between liking and loving. To like someone is to be attracted to him, to be pleased by him, and to want to be with him. To love someone is to have high regard and goodwill for her, to desire what is best for her. In a way, to like someone is an almost involuntary response of the heart. We are attracted to people. We find them pleasing. To love someone, by contrast, is an act of the will, a choice to be lived out in deeds.

Many students, due to scars from their upbringing or their own bad habits, are hard to like. But the teacher committed to character education must not only love the flawed young person, she must keep before her the image of the person that student can become. As Harold S. Hubert put it, "Children need love, especially when they do not deserve it."

A teacher's love is sometimes an act of will. Experiencing this kind of love, students submit to the pushes and pulls of education and character formation because they know "this teacher has my best interests at heart."

Give Your Students Structure

Parents and educators can easily agree that they want students to graduate from school as creative, independent, self-directed, and free individuals. The development of these qualities is a high priority for all concerned. However, generations of educators have confused the process for the product. They have cast aside ideas of order, hard work, and self-discipline and have designed schools around these more personally expressive ideas instead.

Schools committed to character realize that students need structure. This structure reflects Aristotle's advice that children should be in the presence of excellence every day.

Classrooms and schools need to surround students with excellence: excellent music, architecture, stories, and lives.

Teach Your Students How to Be a Friend

Parents are frequently more aware of the importance of friends to students than are teachers. Besides dealing with the constant problem of getting children to come inside for dinner or off the phone and back to their homework, parents are aware of the pain, rarely seen by teachers, that comes with being excluded from a sleepover or dropped by a friend. "Why doesn't anyone like me?" is a question that can break a parent's heart.

The desire for friendship is particularly strong among the current generation of students. Many of them have moved often in their lives. With few roots, they are eager to be accepted. This desire to be with friends and to be liked as a friend does not mean, however, that children naturally know how to be a friend. True friendship is a virtue; it is a way of being. Students often confuse their desire to belong with friendship.

There is much that teachers and administrators can do to stimulate real friendships. Besides exemplifying friendship in their own lives, they can work to create an ethos of friendship. They can directly attack a put-down culture—one in which slurs and insults reign—through a frontal campaign: "That is not the way we do things at Lincoln Middle School." Further, they can teach about friendship. Literature and history are filled with accounts that not only provide examples of friendship but also excite the desire for true friendship.

Learning how to be a good friend is an excellent topic with which to engage students when you are talking with them about the idea of making themselves individuals of character.

Offer Advising Programs

Several schools have initiated advising programs. This works particularly well at the middle and secondary level when students appreciate more mature relationships with adult mentors and teachers. Some schools structure small advising groups, and others establish a one-on-one meeting plan. Here are some important considerations to keep in mind:

- Establish goals for the advising program that will promote the good habits of mind, heart, and action that support both intellectual and character development.

- Establish the time and frequency of advising meetings.

- Develop a set of guidelines for students, parents, and teachers about the role and scope of advising in the students' academic and character development.

Advising should not be confused with professional counseling. Compared to a counselor, an adviser is more a personal coach or mentor for students, offering specific but brief practical advice and support that helps students to identify their strengths and weaknesses, their good habits and bad, and encourages each student to take his or her own life project seriously. Advisers invite students to identify small, achievable goals at the end of each advising meeting and help students articulate realistic action plans for working toward these goals.

▶ Key Thoughts

As educators we need to make learning experiences and goals attractive and meaningful. They must be compelling enough to draw students from competing distractions, such as those offered by popular culture, the entertainment industry, and fashion trends. We need to help students see that external measures of success—such as power, money, and pleasurable amusements—are not a substitute for the internal satisfaction and fulfillment that results from internalizing virtues that endure and enable a person to flourish in a variety of circumstances.

▶ Discussion and Reflection Activities

When we tell students that the reason for taking school seriously or getting a good grade is that it will help them secure a good job or become successful, we teach them to measure the worth of an effort by its monetary or utilitarian outcome. The following activities may assist you to help students develop internal motivation or at least learn to be skeptical of the satisfaction money, power, and mere amusement can bring:

- Make a list of the activities, persons, and possessions you enjoy most in your life. Then put a star next to the items that you value or admire most. Finally, discuss briefly why you starred these items. To what extent is the worth of these starred items a source of money, power, or amusement?

- The next time you discuss with your students a choice made by a character in a story or by a person who figures in history or current events, ask your students what motivated this person's choice. When do choices motivated by power, money, and desire for fun make good choices? When do they constitute a poor choice? Why? (Choices in such works as *Macbeth*, *The Great Gatsby*, *Pinocchio*, the Harry Potter books, and *Sadako and the Thousand Paper Cranes* might be addressed.)

▶ Best Practice Stories

Walnut Hill Elementary in Dallas, uses CHAMPS, a nationwide leadership program, to help its sixth-graders better learn how to work together as a group and serve others. At the beginning of the year the students participate in a workshop to learn what it means to be a champ. IBM, one of the school's sponsors, donates the use of a large conference room for this event. At the end of the training, students are assigned to project groups. Each group meets twice a month; one of the meetings is marked for team-building activities and the other is a workday devoted to the group's particular year-long project. The projects include recycling, working in the library, mentoring younger students, serving the school office by making announcements and maintaining the marquee, recognizing all school birthdays throughout the year with homemade certificates, and running the school store.

"CHAMPS originated as a gang intervention program," says Tricia Taylor, the school counselor. "The idea was, 'Give them a group to belong to and they'll be less likely to look for membership in outside groups.'" At Walnut Hill, the program has helped focus the sixth-graders during their sometimes trying final year as elementary students. "Students know that when they become a sixth-grader, it's their turn to shine and become a role model."

A junior high school near Columbus, Ohio, has a central hallway devoted to pictures and biographies of all the famous men and women who have graduated from the school. The school calls it the Hall of Fame. It helps give students structure by clearly communicating to them that they are part of a tradition and that the people in their community and school expect them to do something with their lives. It provokes in them a sense that they are part of a continuum, that they are expected to be excellent and to do something for others.

At the Benjamin Franklin Classical Charter School, students in grades 6 to 8 are assigned to service teams of ten to twelve students each. Students have the same faculty service team adviser and belong to the same group for all three years. The purpose of these groups is to help students practice the cardinal virtues through engaging in small acts of service related to these virtues. Each month, students select one activity to complete individually. These activities come from *Stepping Stones,* a workbook by Deborah Farmer, and they are organized around the cardinal virtues, which are also the

"In these stern days, young people are searching for meaning, searching for some reason not just to exist but to live.

"They want to do more than cope with existence; they want to have full and worthwhile lives.

"May it be said of each of us who teach that we dared to offer them a vision of the good life . . . in the hope that they would choose it for themselves."

—TONY JARVIS, "Beyond Ethics," *Journal of Education,* 1993, *175*(2), p. 73.

school's core virtues: temperance, justice, fortitude, and prudence. For example, in September, students complete a service activity that relates to justice. In October, they pick one involving temperance. In their eighth-grade year, students work with their adviser on a *capstone project*—a self-designed, long-term service project. Additionally, every year each service team selects projects that the group will work on as a whole, such as cleaning up the yard, recognizing parent volunteers, working with elementary grade classrooms, and tying quilts for shelters. (Appendix I shows the *Stepping Stones* activities for the seventh grade for the virtue of justice.)

Appendices
Part One

Good Ideas

The Character Education Manifesto

> Is there no virtue among us? If there be not, we are in a
> wretched situation. No theoretical checks—no form of govern-
> ment can render us secure. To suppose that any form of gov-
> ernment will secure liberty or happiness without any virtue in
> the people, is a chimerical idea.
>
> —JAMES MADISON, speech at the
> Virginia Ratifying Convention

> To educate a man in mind and not morals is to educate a men-
> ace to society.
>
> —THEODORE ROOSEVELT

AMERICAN SCHOOLS have had from their inception a moral mandate. Moral authority, once vested firmly in both our schools and teachers, has receded dramatically over the past few decades. While many teachers are valiantly working to promote good character in their classrooms, many are receiving mixed and confusing messages. Attempts made to restore values and ethics to the school curriculum through values clarification, situational ethics, and discussion of moral dilemmas have proven both weak and ephemeral, failing to strengthen the character and behavior of our young people. Still our schools too often champion rights at the expense of responsibility, and self-esteem at the expense of self-discipline.

Distressed by the increasing rates of violence, adolescent suicide, teen pregnancy, and a host of other pathological and social ills assaulting American youth, we propose that schools and teachers reassert their responsibility

---

Developed by Kevin Ryan, Karen E. Bohlin, and Judith O. Thayer, the Center for the Advancement of Ethics and Character at Boston University, 1996.

as educators of character. Schools cannot however, assume this responsibility alone; families, neighborhoods, and faith communities must share in this task together. We maintain that authentic educational reform in this nation begins with our response to the call for character. True character education is the hinge upon which academic excellence, personal achievement, and true citizenship depend. It calls forth the very best from our students, faculty, staff, and parents.

We, the undersigned, believe the following guiding principles ought to be at the heart of this educational reform:

1. Education in its fullest sense is inescapably a moral enterprise—a continuous and conscious effort to guide students to know and pursue what is good and what is worthwhile.

2. We strongly affirm parents as the primary moral educators of their children and believe schools should build a partnership with the home. Consequently, all schools have the obligation to foster in their students personal and civic virtues such as integrity, courage, responsibility, diligence, service, and respect for the dignity of all persons.

3. Character education is about developing virtues—good habits and dispositions which lead students to responsible and mature adulthood. Virtue ought to be our foremost concern in educating for character. Character education is not about acquiring the right views—currently accepted attitudes about ecology, prayer in school, gender, school uniforms, politics, or ideologically charged issues.

4. The teacher and the school principal are central to this enterprise and must be educated, selected, and encouraged with this mission in mind. In truth, all of the adults in the school must embody and reflect the moral authority which has been invested in them by the parents and the community.

5. Character education is not a single course, a quick-fix program, or a slogan posted on the wall; it is an integral part of school life. The school must become a community of virtue in which responsibility, hard work, honesty, and kindness are modeled, taught, expected, celebrated, and continually practiced. From the classroom to the playground, from the cafeteria to the faculty room, the formation of good character must be the central concern.

6. The human community has a reservoir of moral wisdom, much of which exists in our great stories, works of art, literature, history, and biography. Teachers and students must together draw from this reservoir both within and beyond the academic curriculum.

7. Finally, young people need to realize that forging their own characters is an essential and demanding life task. And the sum of their school experiences—in successes and failures, both academic and athletic, both intellectual and social—provides much of the raw material for this personal undertaking.

Character education is not merely an educational trend or the school's latest fad; it is a fundamental dimension of good teaching, an abiding respect for the intellect and spirit of the individual. We need to re-engage the hearts, minds, and hands of our children in forming their own characters, helping them "to know the good, love the good, and do the good." That done, we will truly be a nation of character, securing "liberty and justice for all."

Appendix B

Character Education Reading List

Allan, S. *The Way of Water*. Albany: State University of New York Press, 1997.

Aristotle. *Nicomachean Ethics*. (M. Oswald, trans.). Indianapolis: Liberal Arts Press, 1962.

Bellah, R., and others. *Habits of the Heart: Individualism and Commitment in American Life*. San Francisco: HarperSanFrancisco, 1985.

Bellah, R., and others. *The Good Society*. New York: Knopf, 1991.

Bennett, W. J. (ed.). *The Book of Virtues: A Treasury of Great Moral Stories*. New York: Simon & Schuster, 1994.

Bennett, W. J. (ed.). *The Children's Book of Virtues*. New York: Simon & Schuster, 1996.

Bennett, W. J. (ed.). *The Moral Compass: Stories for a Life's Journey*. New York: Simon & Schuster, 1996.

Benninga, J. (ed.). *Moral Character and Civic Education in the Elementary School*. New York: Teachers College Press, 1991.

Brookhiser, R. *Founding Father: Rediscovering George Washington*. New York: Free Press, 1996.

Carter, S. L. *The Culture of Disbelief: How American Law and Politics Trivialize Religious Devotion*. New York: Basic Books, 1993.

Coles, R. *The Moral Life of Children*. Boston: Atlantic Monthly Press, 1986.

Coles, R. *The Call of Stories*. Boston: Houghton Mifflin, 1989.

Collins, M., and Tamarkin, C. *Marva Collins' Way*. Los Angeles: Tarcher, 1990.

Covey, S. *The Seven Habits of Highly Effective Teens*. New York: Franklin Covey, 1998.

Prepared by the Center for the Advancement of Ethics and Character at Boston University.

Damon, W. *The Moral Child.* Cambridge, Mass.: Harvard University Press, 1988.

Damon, W. *Greater Expectations: Overcoming the Culture of Indulgence in America's Homes and Schools.* New York: Free Press, 1995.

Delattre, E. J. *Education and the Public Trust: The Imperative for Common Purposes.* Washington, D.C.: Ethics and Public Policy Center, 1988.

Denby, D. *Great Books.* New York: Simon & Schuster, 1998.

Durkheim, É. *Moral Education: A Study in Theory and Application of the Sociology of Education.* New York: Free Press, 1961.

Durst, M. *Principled Education.* Hayward, Calif.: Principled Academy, 1998.

Eberly, D. (ed.). *The Content of America's Character.* Lanham, Md.: Madison Books, 1995.

Ellenwood, S., McLaren, N., Goldman, R., and Ryan, K. (eds.). *The Art of Loving Well: A Character Education Curriculum for Today's Teenagers.* Boston: Boston University, 1988.

Frankl, V. E. *Man's Search for Meaning.* New York: Simon & Schuster, 1959.

Gauld, J. W. *Character First: The Hyde School Difference.* San Francisco: ICS Press, 1993.

Glendon, M. A., and Blankenhorn, D. *Seedbeds of Virtue: Sources of Competence, Character and Citizenship in American Society.* Lanham, Md.: Madison Books, 1995.

Goodlad, J., Soder, R., and Sirotnik, K. (eds.). *The Moral Dimensions of Teaching.* San Francisco: Jossey-Bass, 1990.

Heath, D. H. *Schools of Hope: Developing Mind and Character in Today's Youth.* San Francisco: Jossey Bass, 1994.

Hibbs, T. *Shows About Nothing.* Dallas: Spence, 1999.

Huffman, H. *Developing a Character Education Program: One School District's Experience.* Washington, D.C.: CEP Clearinghouse, 1995.

Keller, H. *The Story of My Life.* New York: Airmont Books, 1965.

Kidder, T. *Among Schoolchildren.* Boston: Houghton Mifflin, 1989.

Kilpatrick, W. *Why Johnny Can't Tell Right from Wrong.* New York: Simon & Schuster, 1992.

Kilpatrick, W., Wolfe, G., and Wolfe, S. *Books That Build Character: A Guide to Teaching Your Child Moral Value Through Stories.* New York: Simon & Schuster, 1994.

Kozol, J. *Amazing Grace.* New York: Crown, 1995.

Kurtines, W., and Gewirtz, J. L. (eds.). *Handbook of Moral Behavior and Development.* Mahwah, N.J.: Erlbaum, 1991.

Lawrence-Lightfoot, S. *Respect: An Exploration.* Reading, Mass.: Perseus Books, 1999.

Lewis, C. S. *The Abolition of Man.* New York: Macmillan, 1947.

Lewis, H. *A Question of Values.* San Francisco: HarperSanFrancisco, 1990.

Lickona, T. *Educating for Character: How Our Schools Can Teach Respect and Responsibility.* New York: Bantam Books, 1991.

Macintyre, A. *After Virtue.* Notre Dame, Ind.: University of Notre Dame Press, 1984.

Morley, T. *Discipline Through Virtue.* Sugar City, Idaho: ThoMax, 1995.

Noddings, N. *The Challenge to Care in Schools.* New York: Teachers College Press, 1992.

Nucci, L. *Moral Development and Character Education: A Dialogue.* Berkeley, Calif.: McCutchan, 1986.

Palmer, P. J. *The Courage to Teach: Exploring the Inner Landscape of a Teacher's Life.* San Francisco: Jossey-Bass, 1998.

Plato. *Republic.* (G.M.A. Grube, trans.). Indianapolis: Hackett, 1992.

Postman, N. *Amusing Ourselves to Death.* New York: Penguin Books, 1986.

Pritchard, I. *Good Education: The Virtues of Learning.* Norwalk, Conn.: Judd, 1998.

Purpel, D. *The Moral and Spiritual Crisis in Education: A Curriculum for Justice and Compassion.* New York: Bergin & Garvey, 1988.

Ryan, K., and Bohlin, K. *Building Character in Schools.* San Francisco: Jossey-Bass, 1999.

Ryan, K., and Lickona, T. *Character Development in Schools and Beyond.* (2nd ed.) Washington D.C.: Council for Researching Values and Philosophy, 1992.

Sichel, B. *Moral Education: Character, Community and Ideals.* Philadelphia: Temple University Press, 1988.

Sizer, N., and Sizer, T. *The Students Are Watching.* Boston: Beacon Press, 1999.

Sommers, C., and Sommers, F. (eds.). *Vice and Virtue in Everyday Life: Introductory Readings in Ethics.* Orlando, Fla.: Harcourt Brace, 1989.

Taulbert, C. *Eight Habits of the Heart.* New York: Penguin Books, 1997.

Urban, H. *Twenty Things I Want My Kids to Know.* Nashville: Thomas Nelson, 1992.

Vessels, G. G. *Character and Community Development: A School Planning and Teacher Training Handbook.* Westport, Conn.: Praeger, 1998.

Vincent, P. F. *Developing Character in Students.* Chapel Hill, N.C.: New View, 1994.

Vincent, P. F. *Promising Practices in Character Education: Nine Success Stories from Around the Country.* Chapel Hill, N.C.: Character Development Group, 1996.

Wattenberg, B. J. *Values Matter Most.* New York: Free Press 1995.

Welty, E., and Sharp, R. A. (eds.). *The Norton Book of Friendship.* New York: Norton, 1991.

Wiley, L. S. *Comprehensive Character-Building Classroom: A Handbook for Teachers.* DeBary, Fla.: Longwood Communications, 1998.

Wilson, J. Q. *The Moral Sense.* New York: Free Press, 1993.

Wright, R. *The Moral Animal.* New York: Random House, 1994.

Wynne, E., and Ryan, K. *Reclaiming Our Schools: A Handbook on Teaching Character, Academics and Discipline.* Columbus, Ohio: Merrill, 1992.

Appendices
Part Two

Action Strategies

Appendix C

Internalizing Virtue: An Instructional
and Schoolwide Framework

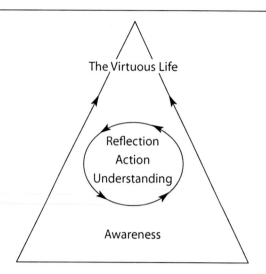

Internalizing Virtue: How It's Done

1. **Awareness** is created as educators and others explain and define virtues, as a means of building a common language and shared character goals for the school community. Students become aware that respect, kindness, and diligence, for example, matter when teachers use these words and remind students of the importance of these virtues to both their intellectual and their personal development.

2. **Understanding** virtue is that "A-ha!" moment for a student when he or she realizes that living virtuously and making wise choices contributes to personal happiness and the happiness of others. Understanding is enlightened through stories, poetry, images, music, film, and examples of lives past and present. Understanding heightens students' desire to lead a virtuous life; to use their time, talent, and energy well; and to make wise choices.

3. **Action** enables us to build good habits. We learn by doing. As Aristotle noted, "[Men] become builders by building and lyre-players by playing the lyre; so too we become just by doing just acts . . . brave by doing brave acts." Action is about putting virtue into practice.

4. **Reflection** involves thinking about what we have done (a thoughtful examination of actions). Was it a good or a bad decision? Why? What would we do differently next time? Reflection helps us develop the self-knowledge essential to internalizing virtue. It cultivates moral reasoning.

   Virtues are those good habits of mind, heart, and action that *enable us to choose and act well.* Fostering virtue—helping students to lead flourishing lives—is at the heart of character education.

Why the Circle Inside the Triangle?

Internalizing virtue isn't just about acquiring a set of habits. It's about gradually gaining wisdom—acting and then reflecting on what we've done, learning from our mistakes, and coming to a greater understanding of how to live a life shaped by such qualities as compassion, respect, and honesty.

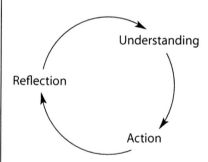

- Our <u>understanding</u> informs our *actions.*
- Our <u>actions</u> give us reason to *reflect.*
- These <u>reflections</u> strengthen our *understanding* of virtue and our commitment to *act* accordingly.

Developed by Karen E. Bohlin, Deborah Farmer, and Kevin Ryan.

Appendix D

100 Ways to Bring Character Education to Life

Building a Community of Virtue

1. Develop a school code of ethics. Distribute it to every member of the school community. Refer to it often. Display it prominently. Make sure all school policy reflects it.

2. Institute a student-to-student tutoring program.

3. Promote schoolwide or intraclass service clubs with real missions to serve the school, class, or external community.

4. Encourage students to identify a charity or in-school need, collect donations, and help administer the distribution of funds.

5. Ensure that the school's recognition systems cover both character and academics.

6. Recognize a variety of achievements, such as surpassing past personal achievements or meeting a predetermined goal.

7. Consistently prohibit gossip and, when appropriate, discuss its damaging consequences.

8. Enforce a zero-tolerance policy on swearing. Prohibit vulgar and obscene language in the classroom and on school property.

9. Use morning announcements, school and classroom bulletin boards, and the school newsletter to highlight the various accomplishments—particularly character-oriented ones—of students and faculty members.

Developed and updated by the staff of the Center for the Advancement of Ethics and Character at Boston University, with input from numerous teachers and administrators.

10. When conflicts arise around the school or class, teach about discretion, tact, and privacy—and about discreetly informing appropriate adults of the conflict.

11. Have students take turns caring for class pets and taking them home over weekends and holidays. Discuss and demonstrate the responsibility required to care for living creatures.

12. Invite student volunteers to clean up their community. With parental support, encourage students to build a community playground, pick up litter, rake leaves, plant trees, paint a mural, remove graffiti, or clean up a local park or beach.

13. Find out the significance behind your school's traditions, and emphasize those that build school unity.

14. Display the school flag. Learn the school song. If you don't have either, have a contest!

15. Have ceremonies to mark the beginning and end of the school year and for teachers and staff members who are leaving.

16. Examine school assemblies. Do a minority of students control the majority of assemblies? How could more students be involved? Are the chants at pep assemblies appropriate? Do they build school spirit without demeaning other schools?

17. Ensure students behave responsibly and respectfully when watching athletic competitions.

18. In physical education and sports programs, place a premium on good sportsmanship. Participation in sports should provide good habits for the life beyond sports.

19. Hang pictures of heroes or heroines in classrooms and halls. Include appropriate explanatory text.

20. Make the school a welcoming place. Can people walking through the school halls get a good idea of what is happening in classrooms? Is the principal frequently visible to students? Are there clear welcome signs prominently placed near the school's main door?

21. Start a school scrapbook with photos, news stories, and memorabilia reflecting the school's history and accomplishments. Involve school members in contributing to and maintaining the collection. Show it off to visitors and new families.

22. Publicly recognize the work of the "unsung heroes" who keep the school running: the custodians, repairmen, secretaries, cafeteria workers, and volunteers.

23. Develop a system of welcoming and orienting new students to the school.

24. Prohibit the display of any gang symbols or paraphernalia on school property. Remove graffiti immediately—including in student bathrooms.

25. Let students take some responsibility for the maintenance and beautification of the school. Classes could "adopt a hallway," shelve misplaced books, plant flowers, and so forth. Post signs identifying caretakers.

Mining the Curriculum

26. Have students do a major paper on a living public figure ("My Personal Hero"), focusing on the moral achievements and virtues of the individual. First, do the groundwork of helping them understand what constitutes a particularly noble life.

27. In history and literature classes, regularly weave in a discussion of motivations, actions, and consequences.

28. Insist that quality matters. Homework should be handed in on time, neat and complete. Details do count.

29. Include the study of "local heroes" in social studies classes.

30. Help students form friendships. When forming cooperative learning groups, keep in mind both the academic and emotional needs of the students. These groups can be an opportunity to group students who might not otherwise interact with one another.

31. Ensure students have a firm understanding of what constitutes plagiarism and of the school's firm policy against it. But, more important, help them understand why it is wrong.

32. Celebrate the birthdays of heroes and heroines with discussions of their accomplishments.

33. Choose the finest children's and adult literature to read with your students—literature rich with meaning and imagery. Don't waste time with mediocre or unmemorable texts.

34. Don't underestimate the power of stories to build a child's moral imagination. Read aloud to students daily.

35. Conduct literature discussions—even in the youngest grades. Ask questions which encourage reflection. Don't immediately jump to the "moral of the story" while ignoring the richness, beauty, or complexity of the text. General questions could include: "What did this book

make you think about or feel?" "Tell me about [a character's name]—what kind of person was he?" "Why do you think the author wrote this book—what did she want to say to the reader?" Don't leave a story, however, without having students grapple with its moral message.

36. Build empathy in literature and social studies classes by teaching children to put themselves in the shoes of the people they are reading about or studying.

37. Read and discuss biographies from all subject areas. Help students identify the person's core or defining characteristics.

38. While studying about great men and women, do not consistently avoid the subject of personal weakness—especially in the upper grades. A study of a person's "whole" character can provide a powerful lesson in discernment and compassion. Consider a thoughtful discussion of the following question: "Can a person be 'great' (and good) and still have some character flaws?"

39. Teach students to write thoughtful letters: thank-you notes, letters to public officials, letters to the editor, and so on.

40. Assign homework that stimulates and challenges students. Engaging and demanding assignments will give rise to self-discipline and perseverance.

41. Set up a buddy reading system between an older and a younger class. Carefully teach the older students techniques that will help make their teaching experiences successful. Impress upon them the responsibility and patience required when helping those who are younger and less skilled in a subject than they are.

42. Have students memorize poetry and important prose selections such as the preamble to the Declaration of Independence or the Gettysburg Address. In the process, make sure they understand the ideas that make these works worthy of committing to memory.

43. In science, address with each unit (when appropriate) the ethical considerations of that field of study. Students need to see that morality and ethics are not confined to the humanities.

44. In math classes, specifically address the habits—such as courage, perseverance, and hard work—required to be a successful math student. Class rules and homework policies should reflect and support these habits.

45. In social studies, examine—and reexamine yearly, if the curriculum affords the chance—the responsibilities of the citizen. What can students do right now to build the habits of responsible citizenship?

Involving Teachers, Administrators, and Staff

46. Choose a personal motto or mission statement.

47. Tell your students who your heroes are and why you chose them.

48. Lead by example. Pick up the piece of paper in the hall. Leave the classroom clean for the next teacher. Say thank you.

49. Employ the language of virtue in conversations with colleagues: responsibility, commitment, perseverance, courage, and so on.

50. Make your classroom expectations clear and hold students accountable.

51. Admit mistakes and seek to make amends. Expect and encourage students to do likewise.

52. Follow through. Do what you say you will do. For example, administer tests when they are scheduled; don't cancel at the last minute after students have prepared.

53. If you engage in community or church service, let your students know, in an appropriate, low-key manner.

54. Illustrate integrity: let students see that you meet the expectations of hard work, responsibility, gratitude, and perseverance that you place upon them.

55. Give students sufficient and timely feedback when you evaluate their work. This demonstrates to students that their work matters and that teachers take an interest in their improvement and success.

56. Teach justice and compassion by helping students separate the doer from the deed.

57. Stand up for the underdog or the student who is being treated poorly by classmates. But use discretion: sometimes use an immediate response; sometimes use a private, small-group meeting—perhaps the person in question ought not be present.

58. Use constructive criticism (individually and collectively), tempered by compassion. Use class discussions as a time to teach students to do the same when responding to one another.

59. Include in faculty and staff meetings and workshops discussions of the school's moral climate. How can the ethos of the school be improved?

60. Begin a bulletin board where teachers and administrators can share their own "100 Ways . . ."

Involving Parents

61. Create a written code of behavior for the classroom and the school. Ask parents to read and sign the code, as a pledge of mutual support.

62. Consider having a parent representative present while developing such school codes.

63. Make the effort to notify parents of student misbehavior, via notes, phone calls, and personal visits.

64. "Catch students being good," and write or call parents to report it.

65. Communicate with parents about appropriate ways they can help students with their schoolwork.

66. Send a letter home to parents before the school year starts, introducing yourself, your classroom, your enthusiasm, and your expectations, particularly your hope that they will help you help their child.

67. Involve as many parents as possible in the parent-teacher organization.

68. Frequently share the school's vision and high ideals for its students with parents.

69. Open a dialogue with parents. They can be a teacher's greatest ally in helping students succeed. They can provide pertinent, invaluable information about their child's academic and social background, interests, talents, difficulties, and so on.

70. In the school newsletter, inform parents of upcoming events, units of study, and opportunities to participate in school and after-school activities.

71. Develop a list of suggested readings and resources in character education, and share it with parents.

72. When appropriate, provide literacy classes or tutors for parents.

73. Provide parents with access to the school library. Provide a suggested reading list of books with solid moral content that make good read-alouds.

74. Structure opportunities for parents to meaningfully participate in classrooms, beyond providing refreshments and chaperoning field trips; for example: reading with students, presenting a lesson in an area of expertise, tutoring, sharing family heirlooms, helping organize class plays or projects.

75. Send out monthly newsletters to parents that include details on your character education efforts.

76. Include anecdotes about commendable student performance in the school newsletter.

77. Include a "parents' corner" in the newsletter, where parents can share parenting tips, book titles, homework helps, and so on.

78. When your school welcomes a new student, welcome the new student's family as well.

79. What can your school do to encourage greater attendance at parent-teacher conferences? Examine the times they are held and how they are advertised. What is being done to reach out to the parents who never come?

80. During parent-teacher conferences, ask parents, "What are your questions or concerns?" Then listen carefully to their answers.

Involving Students

81. Begin a service program in which students "adopt-an-elder" from the community. Arrange opportunities for students to visit, write letters, read to, or run errands for their adoptee.

82. Structure opportunities for students to perform community service.

83. Prohibit students from being unkind or using others as scapegoats in the classroom.

84. Make it clear to students that they have a moral responsibility to work hard in school.

85. Impress upon students that being a good student means far more than academic success.

86. After students have developed an understanding of honesty and academic integrity, consider instituting an honor system for test taking and homework assignments.

87. Provide opportunities for students to both prepare for competition and engage in cooperation.

88. Help students acquire the power of discernment—including the ability to judge the truth, worth, and biases of what is presented on TV, the radio, and the Internet.

89. Invite graduates of the high school to return and talk about their experience in the next stage of life. Ask them to discuss what habits or virtues could make the transition to work or college successful and what bad habits or vices cause problems.

90. Have students identify a substantive quote or anecdote from which they can begin to develop a personal motto.

91. Overtly teach courtesy.

92. Make every effort to instill a work ethic in students. Frequently explain their responsibility to try their best. Create minimum standards for the

quality of work you will accept—then don't accept work that falls short.

93. During election years, encourage students to research candidates' positions, listen to debates, participate in voter registration drives, and if eligible, vote.

94. Use the language of virtue with students—responsibility, respect, integrity, diligence, and so on—and teach them to use this language.

95. In large middle and high schools, assess what is being done to keep students from "falling through the cracks." Every student needs at least one teacher or counselor to take specific interest in him or her.

96. In middle and high schools, consider instituting (or strengthening) an advising program. Advisers should do more than provide job and college information—they should take an interest in the intellectual and character development of their advisees.

97. Hold students accountable to a strict attendance and tardiness policy.

98. Through stories, discussion, and example, teach students about true friendship. Help them recognize the characteristics of true friends and the potentially destructive power of false friendships.

99. Doing the "right thing" is not always an easy choice—especially in the face of peer pressure. Help students, both individually and as a class, to see the long-term consequences of their actions. They may need the support of a responsible adult both before and after choices are made.

100. Remind students—and yourself—that character building is not an easy or one-time project. Fashioning our character is the work of a lifetime.

Appendix E

Friendship and Character in Film

THE FOLLOWING list suggests scenes from films that could be used in units or lessons across the curriculum that deal with themes such as beneficence, taking others seriously, and the four cardinal virtues. Go through this list of film clips and consider how you might use them in making a presentation. Also suggest alternative clips or other ways of making the same or similar points. Think of this as an initial stage in planning a presentation that you yourself might use with students, parents, colleagues, and so forth.

The Pleasure of Beneficence

The Education of Little Tree [1996]

"When you come on something good, first thing to do is share it."

Taking Others Seriously

Forrest Gump [1994]

"The sweetest voice in the wide world."

To Kill a Mockingbird [1960]

"You never really understand a person until you climb into his skin and walk around in it."

The Function of Friends

As Good as It Gets [1997]

"You make me want to be a better man."

Created by Steven S. Tigner, School of Education, Boston University, for the Center for the Advancement of Ethics and Character Summer Teachers Academies.

Four Cardinal Virtues

Courage

Nobody's Fool [1994]

Learning to be brave.

What About Bob? [1991]

Fear of diving.

Wild Hearts Can't Be Broken [1991]

The first horse dive.

Fried Green Tomatoes [1991]

The bee tree.

Star Trek II: The Wrath of Khan [1982]

Friendship's ultimate expression.

Temperance

Pinocchio [1940]

Pleasure Island.

Groundhog Day [1993]

Cultivating virtue.

Justice

Bonfire of the Vanities [1990]

Justice as decency.

Wisdom

Theoretical Wisdom

Stand and Deliver [1988]

"We will begin each class with a quiz."

Practical Wisdom

Anne of Green Gables [1985]

Saving Minnie May.

Productive Wisdom

Mr. Holland's Opus [1995]

The clarinet lesson.

Appendix F

Virtue in Action: A K–8 Guide

Responsibility	What It Looks Like
Grades K–2	Putting toys and books back where they belong
Grades 3–5	Following directions and listening carefully
Grades 6–8	Reading to or tutoring younger students

Courage	What It Looks Like
Grades K–2	Smiling and saying hello to a new student
Grades 3–5	Asking for help or advice from a teacher or parent even when you are afraid to do so
Grades 6–8	Telling your peers to stop doing something that's hurtful or bothersome to someone else

Diligence	What It Looks Like
Grades K–2	Finishing your art project even if you get bored with it
Grades 3–5	Sticking with the assignment you find so difficult
Grades 6–8	Doing homework neatly, completely, and on time

Kindness	What It Looks Like
Grades K–2	Saying please and thank you; sharing toys and materials
Grades 3–5	Welcoming new students; including all students in playground activities
Grades 6–8	Introducing new students to your friends; helping classmates who are struggling to understand a subject you understand well

Respect	What It Looks Like
Grades K–2	Taking turns
Grades 3–5	Cooperating with classmates and listening to what each one has to say
Grades 6–8	Being fair when speaking about others; trying to understand different points of view

Developed by the Center for the Advancement of Ethics and Character at Boston University.

Loyalty	What It Looks Like
Grades K–2	Taking care of the classroom pet and/or plants
Grades 3–5	Including everyone in games at recess
Grades 6–8	Sticking up for a friend or classmate when someone speaks poorly of him or her

Honesty	What It Looks Like
Grades K–2	Telling the truth
Grades 3–5	Keeping your word
Grades 6–8	Gathering information and data before drawing a conclusion

Perseverance	What It Looks Like
Grades K–2	Sticking to a game or activity
Grades 3–5	Working hard to complete a project
Grades 6–8	Learning to concentrate and making the effort to figure things out

Self-Control	What It Looks Like
Grades K–2	Sharing with others
Grades 3–5	Being patient when raising your hand
Grades 6–8	Limiting the number of hours in front of the TV; making a study schedule and following it

Appendix G

Helping Younger Students Understand the Virtue of Respect

THIS PRACTICAL GUIDE to virtue is an example of helping young students to become aware of and understand a single virtue, in this case, respect. It involves asking three questions: What does the virtue look like? What does it sound like? What does it feel like? To begin this discussion, teachers may want to take the lead by giving students an example and then soliciting their ideas.

What does *respect* look like? It looks like ...

- Students listening to each other during class meetings

- Students helping a friend clean up a spill

- A group of students working well together on a class project, even if they aren't friends

- Students sharing lunch with someone who forgot one

- Students raising their hands in class

What does *respect* sound like? Respect sounds like ...

- A compliment

- Clapping after an assembly or performance

- "Please," "Thank you," and "Excuse me." "Can I help you?" and "Are you OK?"

- Students asking others to stop saying things that are mean, vulgar, or hurtful

What does *respect* feel like? Respect feels like ...

- People are really listening when I talk

- I am accepted for who I am

- I can have fun on the playground without being teased
- Friendship

Teachers might also ask students to suggest additional actions that describe what respect looks like in specific settings:

- In the cafeteria
- In the bathroom
- On the playground
- During gym class
- In a meeting with a specialist
- At an assembly

Appendix H

Columbine Elementary, Grades K–5:
Personal and Social Responsibility Standards

Columbine Elementary School, Grades K–5: Personal and Social Responsibility Standards

	Partially Proficient			
	In Progress	Basic	Proficient	Advanced
Practices organizational skills	I rarely have appropriate supplies, which makes it difficult to learn.	I sometimes need reminding to have appropriate supplies.	If I don't have appropriate supplies, I find a solution so learning is not affected.	I consistently have all my supplies.
	I rarely take notes or folders home or return them back to school.	I sometimes need help or reminders to take notes or folders home and return them back to school.	I usually take notes or folders home and return them to school with few reminders.	I consistently take home notes or folders and return them to school.
	I rarely have appropriate books or materials out, which affects my and the class's learning.	I sometimes need help or reminders to have appropriate books and materials out.	I usually have appropriate books and materials out without help or reminders.	I consistently have appropriate books and materials out.
	I rarely clean up my work area or put things away before starting a new task.	I sometimes clean up my work area and put things away before starting a new task.	I usually clean up my work area and put things away before starting a new task.	I consistently clean up my work area and put things away before starting a new task.
	I rarely complete my work and turn it in on time.	I sometimes remember to hand in my completed work, but I need a lot of reminders.	I usually remember to hand in my completed work with few reminders.	I consistently complete my work and remember to hand it in with no reminders.

	Partially Proficient		
	In Progress	**Basic**	**Proficient**	**Advanced**

	In Progress	Basic	Proficient	Advanced
Supports and interacts positively with others	I treat my teachers and classmates in a way that puts them down with the tone of my voice, the words I use and the actions I do.	I need to be reminded occasionally to be respectful to my teachers and classmates. I try to think about how the tone of my voice affects others.	I almost always treat teachers and classmates in a caring and respectful way. I am aware that the tone of my voice affects others, and I usually think before I speak.	I consistently treat my teachers and classmates in a respectful and caring way. I make sure that the tone of my voice does not make others feel put down or hurt.
	When corrected or re-directed, I become angry or resistant (pouting, shouting or shutting down) and refuse to listen to other ways of behaving so I repeat this pattern over and over again.	I am beginning to use conflict resolution strategies that help me treat others with respect.	When I do need reminding, I think of my own strategies, listen to suggestions and try different ways of behaving. I use conflict resolution strategies often.	I also encourage and help others to be successful. I know and use several conflict resolution strategies without being reminded.
	I use words that make my classmates feel bad by criticizing, bragging or excluding them.	I am sometimes aware that the words I use with my classmates make them feel bad but I usually don't know what to do to change my actions.	I am aware when my words hurt others and I know what to do to change my actions.	I am very careful never to allow my words to hurt others. I also help people that I feel are being put down by others.

	Partially Proficient			
	In Progress	**Basic**	**Proficient**	**Advanced**
Is enthusiastic about learning	I rarely participate or ask questions during activities or assignments. I rarely complete tasks or assignments.	I need encouragement to participate in class activities and assignments, to complete tasks and assignments and to ask questions.	I usually participate during class activities and assignments and will ask questions with few or no reminders. I usually complete tasks and assignments.	I consistently participate during class activities or assignments and I ask questions when I need to. I consistently complete tasks and assignments.
	I just do a little work because I'm worried I can't do a good job.	I seldom do extra work for a project or read more about a topic on my own.	Sometimes I get excited about something we are learning and I try to do extra work to make a project better or I read more about it on my own.	I do extra work on projects or activities because I like to learn and make my work of the best possible quality. I ask myself questions about things we are working on and try to find the answers on my own. I suggest ways our class could make an activity more interesting or challenging or have better quality products. I read extra outside books because I get excited about something, I learn in class.

Partially Proficient

	In Progress	Basic	Proficient	Advanced
Takes risks and accepts challenges	I often feel uncomfortable when we learn something new or different, so I ask the teacher for help at each step.	I am occasionally uncomfortable about trying something new.	I don't mind trying something new and difficult. If I need to, I ask my friends or teacher for help. I don't give up.	I am excited to try things that are new and different or that look challenging.
	I often get frustrated right away and give up. I don't try to do the activity at all. I often daydream or just don't do the work I am supposed to.	I try not to give up, but many times I do. I need lots of encouragement and help.	I occasionally become frustrated when attempting a task, but I still try to do the task.	I accept challenges and don't become frustrated. I keep on trying until I succeed.

Partially Proficient

	In Progress	Basic	Proficient	Advanced
Accepts responsibility for behavior	Lots of times I'm not sure whether I have a problem or conflict.	I am beginning to know when I have a problem or conflict, but it's hard for me to figure out how it started.	I sometimes need help in recognizing my part in a problem or conflict, but when it's pointed out to me, I recognize it.	I know when I am involved in a problem or conflict, without an adult or classmate telling me.
	I am surprised when a teacher or a classmate tells me I have a problem.	I might know when I have a problem, but I don't have strategies to solve the problem.	I think about how a problem started and who was involved. I consider many different ways to solve the problems, but I may need more than one chance.	I can figure out how a problem started and can listen to or think of possible solutions.

| | Partially Proficient | | | |
	In Progress	Basic	Proficient	Advanced
	I blame others for my behavior. I don't want to talk about it. It's never my fault. I think things are okay, and they're not.	Sometimes I can think of solutions but I often need an adult to provide suggestions.	I sometimes use my problems or conflicts to figure out how to behave in the future and may need more than one chance to change my behavior.	I am good at solving problems and can use my problems or conflicts to figure out how to behave in the future. I get past my mistakes quickly. I can talk about my behavior without making excuses.
Listens attentively, follows directions, stays on task	I seldom know what to do after directions have been given so I can't begin working.	I sometimes don't know what to do after directions have been given. I might need to be reminded to get to work.	I usually understand the directions and am able to begin work.	I consistently use different strategies to figure out things I don't understand, and am able to begin work immediately.
	I often interrupt when others are speaking.	I sometimes interrupt when others are speaking.	I seldom interrupt when others are speaking. When I do interrupt, I can stop myself.	I rarely interrupt when others are speaking. I also help by reminding others when they are interrupting.
	I am usually distracted and I distract others which prevents learning.	Sometimes I am distracted and distract others which prevents learning.	If I allow myself to be distracted, I get myself back on track with little reminding. I seldom distract others.	I don't need reminders to stay on task. I allow others to do their work by concentrating on completing mine.

Partially Proficient

	In Progress	Basic	Proficient	Advanced
Evaluates own learning	I don't always understand how I completed a task.	Sometimes I can give a reason for the choices I make.	I can give a reason for the choice I've made.	I can give multiple reasons for the choices I make.
	It is hard for me to remember to check my work.	Sometimes I review my work for quality, thoroughness, and effective thinking.	I usually review my work for quality, thoroughness, and effective thinking.	I constantly review my work to check for quality, thoroughness, and effective thinking.
	I cannot tell others what I have learned and I'm not sure myself what I've learned.	When asked, I might be able to think about what I've learned and be able to tell others what I've learned.	I talk about what I've learned. I can identify what I've learned.	I can describe what I've learned and how new learning has changed my thinking.
	I'm not sure how to make my work better.	Sometimes I can see a way to improve my work, but I still need my teacher to tell me what and how to improve what I have done.	I usually can describe how to improve my work and proceed to improve it.	I can describe, in multiple ways, how I can improve my work. I can describe what I learned from my friends. I credit my friends for the ideas I like. I can identify gaps in my knowledge about something.

Reprinted with the permission of Principal Michael Galvin, Columbine Elementary School, Woodland Park, Colorado.

Appendix I

Stepping Stone Activities for Grade 7: Justice

> **Justice means treating others with respect and taking responsibility for their well-being; fairness.**
>
> *Related Traits*
> Respect · Kindness
> Friendship · Generosity · Fairness
>
> 1. For two weeks, make an extra effort to treat others with respect. Before you begin, list two specific ways in which you could do this (for example, saying thank you to each person who helps you in a day or refraining from making any comment that puts down someone else). When you finish, describe the results on a reflections page. (Respect)
>
> _____   _____   _____
> Student Signature/Date   Parent Signature/Date   Adviser Signature/Date
>
> 2. Your seven years in school have taught you a few things! Share this knowledge by tutoring a younger student for fifteen to twenty minutes twice a week for two weeks. Lower grade teachers may be able to suggest to you students who could use the extra help in reading, writing, or math. (Remember to obtain permission from the student's parents first.) (Generosity)
>
> _____   _____   _____
> Student Signature/Date   Parent Signature/Date   Adviser Signature/Date
>
> 3. One way to show respect to teachers and younger students is to assist in their classrooms. Volunteer your services to a teacher for three lunch periods and/or study halls this month. Arrange in advance both what you will be working on and when. (Respect)
>
> _____   _____   _____
> Student Signature/Date   Parent Signature/Date   Adviser Signature/Date

---

Reprinted from Deborah Farmer and others, *Stepping Stones* (workbook), 2001.

4. Research shows that children who are read to are much more likely to succeed in school. Share your knowledge by reading to a child at least four times this month. Carefully choose stories and books that you think this child would enjoy. (Generosity)

_____   _____   _____
Student Signature/Date   Parent Signature/Date   Adviser Signature/Date

5. The desk or table you sit at is used six hours a day, five days a week. Think about it. Volunteer to do a midyear desk cleaning for one or more teachers in the school. Locate cleaning supplies and arrange a convenient time with the teacher you want to help. (Generosity)

_____   _____   _____
Student Signature/Date   Parent Signature/Date   Adviser Signature/Date

6. Pre-arrange to set up chairs for one or more evening events at the school this month. Use the school calendar as your guide, and contact the person in charge of this event to offer your services. (Generosity)

_____   _____   _____
Student Signature/Date   Parent Signature/Date   Adviser Signature/Date

7. While it's fun the first few times, shoveling snow gets old quickly—especially for those who are elderly or who lead busy lives. This winter, shovel a neighbors' driveway or walk-way—without getting caught! (Kindness)

_____   _____   _____
Student Signature/Date   Parent Signature/Date   Adviser Signature/Date

8. Simple tasks like vacuuming, dusting, and mowing the lawn become difficult with age or illness. Spend an afternoon doing housework or yard work for someone who could use a helping hand. (Generosity)

_____   _____   _____
Student Signature/Date   Parent Signature/Date   Adviser Signature/Date

Appendix J

Benjamin Franklin Classical Charter School
Discipline Reflection Form

Grades 6–8

Name: _____   Date: _____

Grade/Homeroom Teacher: _____

When you violate one of the school's core expectations, you take a step backward. This sheet is designed to help you regain your footing. Answer the following questions thoughtfully and in complete sentences.

1. What happened? (In detail)

_____
_____
_____
_____
_____
_____
_____
_____

2. Why was this a poor decision? *Whom did it affect?*

_____
_____
_____
_____
_____
_____
_____
_____

Reprinted by permission of the Benjamin Franklin Classical Charter School.

3. What, specifically, could you have done differently to avoid this mistake? What could you do in the future to make a better decision?

    _____
    _____
    _____
    _____
    _____
    _____
    _____
    _____

4. Which of the following expectations apply to this specific incident? Please check.

☐ Show respect to all members of the school community.

☐ Complete work on time and to the best of your ability.

☐ Arriving on-time to school and individual classes.

☐ Follow school and classroom rules.

☐ Participate in school activities in a way that strengthens yourself and others.

☐ Justice: Treating others the way you would like to be treated.

☐ Temperance: Exercising self-control in speech and actions.

☐ Fortitude: Being willing to stand up for what's right.

☐ Prudence: Using your best judgment to make decisions; living honestly.

Student Signature: _____   Date: _____

Appendix K

Sample Survey of Perceived School Environment: For Teachers, Parents, and Students

THIS THREE-PART SURVEY was created to give those in the school community greater ownership of their environment and what occurs in it. This process of reflection and self-assessment can be adapted to relate to your school's core virtues or set of academic, personal, and social standards.

Perceived School Environment: Teacher Survey

Please check one box for each statement to indicate your level of agreement with the following statements about the school environment: Strongly Agree (SA), Agree (A), Neutral (N), Disagree (D), or Strongly Disagree (SD).

	SA	A	N	D	SD
1. The school is a good place to learn.	☐	☐	☐	☐	☐
2. Students and teachers talk about character development together.	☐	☐	☐	☐	☐
3. Students and teachers reflect upon developing habits of good character.	☐	☐	☐	☐	☐
4. Students use good manners in their speech (such as saying please, thank you, and excuse me).	☐	☐	☐	☐	☐
5. Students turn in their homework on time and it is neatly done.	☐	☐	☐	☐	☐
6. Students take good care of school property (such as books, computers, desks).	☐	☐	☐	☐	☐
7. The playground is an inviting, clean place in which students can play safely.	☐	☐	☐	☐	☐
8. The bathrooms are safe, clean, and in working condition.	☐	☐	☐	☐	☐
9. Families are closely involved in the school.	☐	☐	☐	☐	☐
10. Community members are closely involved in the school.	☐	☐	☐	☐	☐
11. Our students return books to the library on time.	☐	☐	☐	☐	☐

	SA	A	N	D	SD
12. Our students speak and act with courtesy while waiting their turn in line.	☐	☐	☐	☐	☐
13. Our students are honest.	☐	☐	☐	☐	☐
14. Our students cooperate with each other.	☐	☐	☐	☐	☐
15. Teachers at this school work well together.	☐	☐	☐	☐	☐
16. Teachers at this school talk about students in a positive way.	☐	☐	☐	☐	☐
17. Teachers at this school respect one another.	☐	☐	☐	☐	☐

Perceived School Environment: Student Survey

Please check one box per statement to indicate how often the following things happen at your school: Always, Most of the Time (M), Sometimes (S) Not Often (NO), or Never.

	Always	M	S	NO	Never
1. I learn a lot at this school.	☐	☐	☐	☐	☐
2. I feel safe in this school.	☐	☐	☐	☐	☐
3. I feel good about myself in school.	☐	☐	☐	☐	☐
4. My parents are interested in what happens at school.	☐	☐	☐	☐	☐
5. Teachers are kind in this school.	☐	☐	☐	☐	☐
6. Students act responsibly by turning in their homework assignments on time.	☐	☐	☐	☐	☐
7. Students show respect for others by saying please and thank you.	☐	☐	☐	☐	☐
8. Students show self-discipline by waiting quietly in line.	☐	☐	☐	☐	☐
9. Students are kind to each other.	☐	☐	☐	☐	☐
10. Students take turns, include one another on the playground, and they are friendly to one another in the hallways and in the cafeteria.	☐	☐	☐	☐	☐
11. Students are honest.	☐	☐	☐	☐	☐
12. Students cooperate with each other.	☐	☐	☐	☐	☐
13. Students are dependable.	☐	☐	☐	☐	☐
14. I like coming to school.	☐	☐	☐	☐	☐

Perceived School Environment: Parent Survey

Please check one box per statement to indicate your level of agreement with the following statements about the school environment: Strongly Agree (SA), Agree (A), Neutral (N), Disagree (D), or Strongly Disagree (SD).

	SA	A	N	D	SD
1. The school is a good place to learn.	☐	☐	☐	☐	☐
2. Students and teachers talk about character development together.	☐	☐	☐	☐	☐
3. Students and teachers reflect upon developing habits of good character.	☐	☐	☐	☐	☐
4. Students use good manners in their speech (such as saying please, thank you, and excuse me).	☐	☐	☐	☐	☐

	SA	A	N	D	SD
5. Students turn in their homework on time, and it is neatly done.	☐	☐	☐	☐	☐
6. Students take good care of school property (such as books, computers, desks).	☐	☐	☐	☐	☐
7. The playground is an inviting, clean place in which students can play safely.	☐	☐	☐	☐	☐
8. The bathrooms are safe, clean, and in working condition.	☐	☐	☐	☐	☐
9. Families are closely involved in the school.	☐	☐	☐	☐	☐
10. I feel that my input is respected at this school.	☐	☐	☐	☐	☐
11. My voice is heard by teachers and administrators when I have a problem.	☐	☐	☐	☐	☐
12. Students at this school are honest.	☐	☐	☐	☐	☐
13. I feel welcome when I visit this school.	☐	☐	☐	☐	☐
14. Teachers in this school treat children with respect.	☐	☐	☐	☐	☐
15. Students at this school cooperate with each other.	☐	☐	☐	☐	☐
16. Teachers at this school talk about students in a positive way.	☐	☐	☐	☐	☐
17. Teachers at this school respect one another.	☐	☐	☐	☐	☐
18. The school is safe.	☐	☐	☐	☐	☐

Appendices
Part Three

Curriculum

Appendix L

The Great Depression: Learning Courage and Hope

Grades 6–9

Awareness

After two lessons on the 1929 stock market crash and its domino effect on the U.S. economy, ask the students to compare the following two quotations:

We are at the end of our rope. There is nothing more we can do.

—Herbert Hoover

I pledge to you, I pledge to America a new deal. We will emerge from these dark days stronger than we were before . . . there is nothing to fear but fear itself.

—Franklin Delano Roosevelt

Ask students to reflect on which sentiment they would prefer in a president. Why? What would be their reaction to a president who said: "Life is great! Everyone in the country is doing fine!" Discuss the meaning of *hope.* Certainly it doesn't involve being blind to present reality, even bleak reality. So what is hope?

Understanding

1. Assist students to gain a deeper understanding of the people who shaped this era by asking them to study Dorothea Lange's photographs, listen to Woody Guthrie ballads, and watch the original recording of the song "God Bless America."

2. Have students read the prize-winning, young adult biography of Eleanor Roosevelt: *Eleanor Roosevelt: A Life of Discovery,* by Russell Freedman. This book provides an alternate window into Depression-era life and politics and shows students a model of true courage. Orphaned at an early age, Eleanor spent her childhood riddled with self-doubt and severe anxiety: "Looking back it strikes me that my childhood and my early youth

were one long battle against fear." Students can trace patterns in her personal development; each time she began to feel consumed by hurt or inadequacy, she reached out to others in need in extraordinary ways. She gained strength from personal tragedy and put herself to use easing the burdens of others.

Action

1. *Oral history.* Over the course of the unit, have students conduct at least one oral history with a person who experienced life in the 1930s. Students should be prepared to craft their questions carefully so that they will hear about several aspects of life during this time, from culture to schooling to politics.

2. *Optimism challenge.* While students study FDR's presidency—including the galvanizing effect of his optimism on many segments of the American population—challenge them to spend one day being "purely positive." On this day, students are not allowed to express negative sentiments in speech or body language.

Reflection

1. *Oral history essay.* After students have completed their interviews, ask them to write an essay describing what they learned about the Great Depression. They are urged to think about what they will tell their grandchildren about what they learned, because future generations will not have the opportunity to interview living witnesses.

2. *Optimism challenge "day after."* The day following the optimism challenge, encourage students to reflect on how their attitude affected the people they came in contact with. Ask them to reflect on the sentiment expressed by Holocaust survivor Viktor Frankl that the last of human freedoms is the freedom to choose one's reaction to any given situation.

3. *Discussion question.* Ask students to discuss this question: FDR's bout with polio left him crippled. Do you think this helped or hindered his abilities as president during the Great Depression? Then ask them to reflect on this statement by FDR's wife, Eleanor: "Franklin's illness proved a blessing in disguise for it gave him strength and courage he had not had before. He had to think out the fundamentals of living and learn the greatest of all lessons—infinite patience and never-ending persistence."

Appendix M

Sojourner's Example: Developing Courage

Grade 5

Biography of Sojourner Truth

Sojourner Truth acted as a strong proponent of equal rights for all African Americans and women. She was born a slave to Colonel Ardinburgh, a man of the Low Dutch class in Ulster County, New York, and was given the birth name of Isabella Baumfree. The name *Baumfree* means "tree" in Low Dutch; she was named after her father who was very tall and straight. Isabella was six feet tall by the time she was thirteen! When she was a young girl, she was sold for one hundred dollars to a new master who spoke only English. The fact that he spoke English and she spoke only Dutch proved to be a problem because she did not understand any of his commands. He would take her to the barn and beat her with a bundle of rods that had been in the fire. He tied her hands and beat her until her skin was lacerated and blood flowed from the wounds.

She was sold several other times during her life and eventually married a slave named Thomas; they had five children. She proved to be a great example of honesty and diligence for her children as they saw her work as a field hand, milkmaid, cleaning woman, weaver, cook, and wet nurse.

When slavery ended in New York in 1827, she was freed but found out that her son Peter had been sold to a Southerner illegally. Isabella challenged this and was the first black woman to sue a white man and win. This is one of the many demonstrations of her courage and determination.

Isabella's mother had a great religious impact on her and taught her that God lived in the sky and watched over all. If she were ever in trouble or in need of help, she only needed to call on God. This spiritual message became

Developed by Mary Worlton, sixth-grade language arts block teacher and character education coordinator, Thomas Hart Middle School, Pleasanton Unified School District, California.

very important to Isabella, and she felt that she needed to share it with others. Isabella changed her name to Sojourner Truth because she was to travel up and down the land declaring truth to people. It is by this name that she is known today.

She left New York on foot in 1843 and walked to Massachusetts where she met Oliver Gilbert, the man who wrote her story, *The Narrative of Sojourner Truth: A Northern Slave.* This book and her presence as a speaker made her a sought-after figure on antislavery and woman's rights circuits. She traveled to and gave speeches in twenty-one states.

Sojourner never learned to read or write, but her speeches were direct and full of common sense, homey metaphors, and biblical allusions. Her most famous speech was given at the Women's Rights Conference in Akron, Ohio, in 1851. Some of the people attending this conference were advocates of women's rights and some were in strong opposition. Many of these same people did not like African Americans, but despite the snickers and rude comments from the audience Sojourner walked up to the podium, straightened up to her six-foot-tall frame, and began to speak. The audience immediately fell silent. She spoke in deep tones, which, though not loud, reached every ear in the house. She delivered her famous "Ain't I a Woman?" speech to a crowd of people who said that women weren't intelligent enough to vote and denied giving them equal rights. But Sojourner had something significant to say to this crowd. She was not afraid to share it.

Sojourner was a very courageous, hardworking, determined woman who dedicated her life to reform. She is a wonderful example of someone who lived a courageous life by standing up for something that was right.

Awareness

1. After students read Sojourner Truth's biography, discuss the life of Sojourner Truth and her influence on civil rights and women's suffrage.

Questions for Students

- What descriptive words would you use to describe Sojourner's personality?

- What do you consider to be Sojourner's greatest accomplishment? Explain.

- Who do you think had the greatest impact on Sojourner? Why?

- What cultural and social situations had a great impact on Sojourner? Why?

- What do Sojourner's actions tell you about her morals and values?

- What were some of the things that Sojourner might have been afraid of?

2. Explain the background circumstances of Sojourner's life and times. She knew that she had to do something about the injustices she felt in spite of the many odds against her. By speaking out with honest feeling, she displayed courage.

3. Discuss how Sojourner displayed courage through traveling around the country giving speeches about the cause she believed in.

Questions for Students

- Do you think she had to overcome any fears?

- If you were asked to do what she did, what might you be afraid of? [Public speaking, being laughed at, being treated with cruelty, having one's children taken away.]

- What does it mean to be courageous? [Courage is the ability to overcome or endure difficulties, including pain, inconvenience, setbacks, or worry. Courage is the habit of overcoming fears by facing them rather than avoiding them. Courage is learning how to solve problems.]

4. Explain how Sojourner was able to express her ideas and frustrations to people in an effective way because she was a powerful speaker. It is important to be able to verbalize thoughts and deliver them clearly to others.

Understanding

Read Sojourner's "Ain't I a Woman" speech aloud. Discuss point by point what she said and why it was effective. Detail the circumstances surrounding the speech first, so students can see how courageous she was.

Ain't I a Woman?

That man over there says that women need to be helped into carriages, and lifted over ditches, and have the best place everywhere. Nobody ever helps me into carriages, or over mud-puddles, or gives me any best place! And ain't I a woman?

Look at me! Look at my arm! I have ploughed and planted, and gathered into barns, and no man could head me! And ain't I a woman? I could work as much and eat as much as a man—when I could get it—and bear the lash as well! And ain't I a woman?

I have borne thirteen children, and seen most all sold off to slavery, and when I cried out with my mother's grief, none but Jesus heard me! And ain't I a woman?

Obliged to you for hearing me, and now old Sojourner ain't got nothing more to say.

Questions for Students

- What do you think about Sojourner's speech?
- How strongly did she believe in what she was saying? How do you know?
- Was this a good speech? Why or why not?
- What is the point she is trying to get across? Which of her examples are most effective in doing this?
- What do you think it means to be courageous?
- How and why was Sojourner courageous?

Action

Discuss the importance of courageous acts in the lives of your students. (It takes courage to speak out for something you think is right even if it is an unpopular choice among your friends, it takes courage to ask someone for forgiveness when you've done something wrong, it takes courage to be friendly to new people, and it takes courage to admit that you need help with something.)

Questions and Activities for Students

- Looking at Sojourner's example as a traveling orator, write a speech about courage and deliver it to the class. [Remind students of the things that made Sojourner's speech so effective and encourage them to implement the same public speaking skills. Give clear examples, stand up tall, speak clearly, and so on.]
- Memorize Sojourner's "Ain't I a Woman" speech and deliver it with her same dramatic zeal!

Reflection

Sojourner was very thoughtful and honest. Encourage students to spend time reflecting on a truly courageous act and explore how they can become more courageous. Have students write a personal goal for acting courageously.

Questions for Students

- What do you think it means to be courageous? Give an example of a courageous act that you have either done yourself or seen someone else do. Be sure to offer enough background information, so your audience is aware of the need for courage.
- Discuss Sojourner Truth's courage. Has it made an impact on you?

Appendix N

Peppe the Lamplighter: Envisioning Diligence
Grade 2

Awareness

The day or week before reading *Peppe the Lamplighter,* by Elisa Bartone, read the students Shel Silverstein's poem "Sarah Cynthia Sylvia Stout Would Not Take the Garbage Out." In their Class Meeting Notebook, have students respond in art and writing to the question: What would this classroom be like if nobody cleaned anything or did any work?

Understanding and Reflection

1. Ask the students these questions:

- Why did Peppe have to work?

- Why was Peppe's father upset about Peppe's new job?

- The author talks a lot about light and dark in this book. What things are light? (The streetlamps when they are lit; Peppe's eyes when he is proud of his work.) What are the streets like when they are dark?

2. Look through the pictures again with the class, noticing the intense color contrasts. Pause on the page that reads:

Each evening at twilight Peppe took the long stick of the lamplighter and passed through the streets. He reached high for the first streetlamp, poked open the glass, and set the lamp aflame. Then one by one he lit them all— and each one Peppe imagined to be a small flame of promise for the future.

Read this passage aloud, look at the picture of the little light lighting a large dark street, and ask: What is the author trying to say? What is a "small flame of promise for the future?"

3. Talk about Peppe's relationship with his sister, Assunta.

4. The people in the city didn't realize how important Peppe's job was until he failed to light the lamps one night. Ask the students: Can you think of any diligent "unsung heroes" in our community? People who aren't famous but make our lives better because of their hard work? (There are numerous possibilities: mail carriers, garbage collectors, nurses, custodians, parents, firefighters, police officers, crossing guards, foster parents, the school secretary, and so forth.) After each suggestion, ask the children to brainstorm what life would be like if these people did not diligently do their jobs.

Action

1. From the list of diligent unsung heroes the class generated, choose, as a class, a person or group of people to whom the class will write letters of appreciation. These letters should be edited and revised before they are delivered.

2. Work with the children to memorize all or a condensed version of "Sarah Cynthia Sylvia Stout . . ." Perhaps each child (or pair of children) could be assigned a couplet to memorize. At the end of the month—or once the poem is at "performance level"—perform the piece for other classes in the school.

SARAH CYNTHIA SYLVIA STOUT WOULD NOT TAKE
THE GARBAGE OUT

Sarah Cynthia Sylvia Stout
Would not take the garbage out!
She'd scour the pots and scrape the pans,
Candy the yams and spice the hams,
And though her daddy would scream and shout,
She simply would not take the garbage out.
And so it piled up to the ceilings:
Coffee grounds, potato peelings,
Brown bananas, rotten peas,
Chunks of sour cottage cheese.
It filled the can, it covered the floor,
It cracked the window and blocked the door
With bacon rinds and chicken bones,
Drippy ends of ice cream cones,
Prune pits, peach pits, orange peel,
Gloppy glumps of cold oatmeal,
Pizza crusts and withered greens,

Soggy beans and tangerines,
Crusts of black burned buttered toast,
Gristly bits of beefy roasts . . .
The garbage rolled on down the hall,
It raised the roof, it broke the wall . . .
Greasy napkins, cookie crumbs,
Globs of gooey bubble gum,
Cellophane from green baloney,
Rubbery blubbery macaroni,
Peanut butter, caked and dry,
Curdled milk and crusts of pie,
Moldy melons, dried-up mustard,
Eggshells mixed with lemon custard,
Cold french fries and rancid meat,
Yellow lumps of Cream of Wheat.
At last the garbage reached so high
That finally it touched the sky.
And all the neighbors moved away,
And none of her friends would come to play.
And finally Sarah Cynthia Stout said,
"OK, I'll take the garbage out!"
But then, of course, it was too late . . .
The garbage reached across the state,
From New York to the Golden Gate.
And there, in the garbage she did hate,
Poor Sarah met an awful fate,
That I cannot right now relate
Because the hour is much too late.
But children, remember Sarah Stout
And always take the garbage out![1]

       —Shel Silverstein

Appendix O

Developing a Yearlong Theme: Our Choices Reveal Our Character

Grade 5

Awareness

On the first day of school, invite two volunteers to the front of the room to act out the following scenarios *without speaking* (body language only).

> Scenario 1. *Last year these two students had a "falling out." The situation escalated through false rumors and mutual backbiting. At this point they go out of their way to avoid meeting each other. On this particular morning, each student has been sent on an errand by his or her teacher. The hallway is narrow, and they cannot avoid passing each other in the hall. What does this encounter look like?*

> Scenario 2. *It's the first day of school. These two students have been friends for years, nearly inseparable. However, one of the students spent the entire summer at his or her grandparents' house in a different state. The students haven't seen each other for almost three months, but now they spot each other across the hall. What does this meeting look like?*

Reflection

After each scenario, discuss what happened with the other students in the class, asking these questions:

- What did you notice?
- What did you notice about their faces, posture, eyes, body positioning? How did they communicate their emotions?
- What did you notice about their hands?

Students acting out these scenarios nearly always ball up their fists, close in their shoulders, and narrow their mouths and eyes for the first scenario. In contrast, students nearly always keep their hands open wide for a wave or high-five in the second scenario.

Understanding

1. Post and read aloud the following poem:

Choose

The single clenched fist lifted and ready,
Or the open asking hand held out and waiting.
Choose:
For we meet by one or the other.[1]

                —Carl Sandburg

2. After reading the poem aloud two or three times, pose the following questions:

- What images do you see in this poem? [Consider having students physically illustrate different ways to make a clenched fist and an open hand.]

- Look at the first line. "Ready" for what?

- Look at the second line. What could the hand be "asking" for? What could it be "waiting" for?

- What does it mean to meet someone with an "open . . . hand"?

- What does it mean to meet someone with a "clenched fist"?

- Do you agree with Sandburg's last two lines: "Choose:/for we meet by one or the other"? Are there options in between?

- Notice that Sandburg implies that we choose *before* the meeting. Can you think of situations when people have chosen in advance to meet somebody with a "clenched fist"?

Action

1. Give the poem immediacy and practicality by having students brainstorm specific ways they show an open hand to others at school. How can we show an open hand to new students? On the playing field? During class discussion? What does showing a clenched fist look like in the classroom and hallways?

2. Consider using one or more of these optional activities:

- Have students trace their open hand on construction paper and write one way in which they can show an open hand to their classmates. Post these around the room.

- Make a list of the ways students found to show an open hand. Use this list to create a set of classroom rules and expectations for student interaction and classroom discussion. Have students specifically practice the actions on this list in the upcoming days.

The teacher keeps the poem on a bulletin board for the remainder of the year as a perennial reminder to choose wisely and treat others with respect. Students are asked to look for manifestations of this theme as they study history and literature. (What are characters "bringing" to their interactions with each other? When has a clenched fist attitude affected politics, war, and social justice?)

On the first day of school the teacher has developed a meaningful theme that will instruct both academics and the classroom environment for the remainder of the year.

Appendix P

Elizabeth Barker, Prison Educator: Thinking About Choice

Grades 9 and 10; also appropriate for a group of teachers

Ask students or teachers to read the following newspaper article and then answer either the questions for students or the questions for teachers.

Ex-inmates owe success to "Ma"

Say teacher gave dignity, direction

Farah Stockman

To the fidgeting students in her extraordinary classroom—whose arms bulged with muscles, scars, and tattoos—Boston University professor Elizabeth "Ma" Barker recited poetry. To her improbable group of scholars, who did their homework in prison cells, Barker brought big-name lecturers like Nobel Prize–winning biochemist George Wald, radio host Christopher Lydon, and radical historian Howard Zinn.

Since Barker started Boston University's prison education program at MCI-Norfolk in 1972, no formal follow-up has been done on what has become of the 187 inmates who earned bachelor's and master's degrees.

But news of Barker's death last month at the age of 89 has stirred the program's scattered alumni to resurface. In paying tribute to her memory at a memorial service and in telephone calls afterward, they also opened a window into what some of the former prisoner-scholars are doing now.

Richard Marinick, once part of a South Boston armored-car robbery ring, is now a tunnel worker on the Big Dig and an aspiring novelist. Robert Heard, who served 13 years for manslaughter, runs a job training program for Pine Street Inn. Joe Loya, a former bank robber, is now married and associate editor of Pacific News Service in San Francisco.

"She turned thugs into poetry-reciting, thinking human beings," said one of Barker's former students who went on to earn his law degree

after being released in 1978. Now a Boston defense lawyer, he asked that his name not be used. "I always thought I had plenty of time to find her and go thank her. I was always waiting for that one big case that would allow me to have serious money so that I could go to BU and say to them, 'Take $10,000, and do something with it in her name.'"

Of course, not everyone who called the four walls of MCI-Norfolk their alma mater became a success. After his release, Bob Heffernan, a favorite student, died of a cocaine overdose.

But "Ma" Barker, affectionately nicknamed after the fugitive and folk hero who led a band of outlaws during the Great Depression, created a community of academics and convicts that few who were members will ever forget.

"It changed the way we can imagine ourselves," Loya said by telephone from California.

"We came in shackles and we left free men," said Heard, a former Black Panther who wound up in prison for manslaughter after fatally shooting a man in a Dorchester dance club.

Heard recalled how Barker believed that the only degree fit for "civilized men" was a liberal arts diploma, something he had considered an aristocratic luxury until he decided to while away some prison hours by taking a drama class from her.

Although he was first skeptical of the elderly white woman who guzzled coffee, spouted poetry, and chain-smoked Chesterfields, Heard eventually became one of her most beloved students. He ultimately coordinated the education program from inside the prison—meeting with BU president John Silber—and ended up bunking for a time at Barker's home in Brookline after he was released.

"In prison you are almost invisible," Heard recalled from his Harrison Avenue office, where he runs a job training program for the homeless that he designed himself. "You can approach a checkpoint and the guard will ask, 'Do you have anything in your pockets?' It matters not what you respond. If you say no, he's going to search your pockets. If you say yes, he's going to search your pockets. But to people like Silber and Elizabeth, we were students and what we said mattered."

Built in 1927, MCI-Norfolk's cluster of dormitories around a grass quad was modeled to look more like a college campus than a medium-security penitentiary. It's known as the only place where inmates could fry a burger in their own kitchen. Spots at MCI-Norfolk had long been coveted, but in 1972 prisoners began to ask for transfers there for another reason: the prison's famous quiz bowl team, and Ma Barker's college classes.

For many of the aging alumni of MCI-Norfolk, the glory days of their enlightenment began in the late '60s, with an inmate named Arthur Devlin, who spent his years on death row memorizing questions and answers from television quiz shows. Devlin started a quiz team that became so successful it vanquished Ivy League challengers and earned a spot on Walter Cronkite's news show. (The only quiz team member to decline the TV appearance was a skittish Mafia gunman.)

Devlin's story impressed Barker, who led a group of BU students to go up against the Norfolk prisoners.

After the duel of wits, Barker was so taken with the prisoner-scholars that she offered to teach them a college course. With the help of Carlo Geromini, a teacher based at the prison, Barker drafted a group of professors into starting a permanent college degree program in the prison.

Today, the program operates in MCI-Norfolk, MCI-Framingham, and Bay State Correctional Center. Over the years, it has offered 425 classes to thousands of inmates, according to program coordinator Robert Cadigan.

On the confidential list of nearly 200 inmates who have fulfilled the requirements to earn degrees are at least three lawyers, one head librarian, a few youth counselors, and a television actor, recounts Geromini.

For Marinick, a former cocaine addict who once ran with a South Boston gang, Barker's program was the difference between being the "caveman" he was in 1984 and the tunnel worker and aspiring writer he is today.

"My thesis was entitled 'Imagination and the Way to Write for Children,'" said Marinick, who was sentenced to 18–20 years for robbing armored cars and firing a pump shotgun at Malden police as he tried to escape arrest. Of his master's thesis, a 119-page compilation of children's stories that earned him a summa cum laude distinction, Marinick said: "It forced me to look at myself, and it forced me to examine society as a whole, not necessarily as the enemy."

By the time Loya, the former bank robber who was raised in the barrios of Los Angeles, got to the classrooms of Norfolk, Barker had already become "a myth," a frail wisp of a grandmother who only occasionally stopped in for poetry readings.

Still, Loya's voice soars when he speaks with reverence about the program she founded, recalling his favorite class: oceanography.

"You had to remember all these things about life in the sea, and different soils and the earth. It's very tedious," said Loya. "But what it gave me was one of the metaphors that I have used since I came out. It allowed me to think of my depth, the landscape of my soul, with more complexity."

Loya recalls getting so frustrated by his first writing assignment that he wanted to hit his teacher in the face. The class forced him to learn self-control.

At a recent Quaker-style memorial service for Barker held in BU's Marsh Chapel, Lydon praised Barker's near-religious belief in the power of education. Another colleague read a statement from Silber. One of Barker's granddaughters played the violin.

Not all her former students could make it on such short notice. Marinick was in Florida, showing his brother the rough draft of a new novel. Another former student was in jail that afternoon, not as an inmate, but as a lawyer interviewing his client.

But seated together in the pews were two white-haired men who whispered and reminisced about the glory days. Quiz bowl captain Devlin, 76, sat next to his old quiz bowl coach, Geromini, 72. One pardoned and the other retired, they discussed the need to send copies of Barker's obituary to the dozens of former students remaining "inside."[1]

Why Is Choice Important? Questions for Students

Ask the students or teachers to read the following quotations. After they read each one, have them use the questions that follow to reflect on the importance of the various choices made by the former inmates described in the newspaper article.

You don't get to choose how you're going to die. Or when. You can only decide how you're going to live.

—Joan Baez

- The former inmates described in this article chose how they were going to live. What decisions did they make? How did these decisions (whether good or bad) change their lives?

So many people walk around with a meaningless life. They seem half-asleep, even when they're busy doing things they think are important. This is because they're chasing the wrong things. The way you get meaning into your life is to devote yourself to loving others, devote yourself to your community around you, and devote yourself to creating something that gives you purpose and meaning.[2]

—Morrie Schwartz

- What had the inmates been chasing originally? What was the result? With Ma's help, what did they begin to chase? What was the result of this choice?

- How did the inmates devote themselves to creating something that gave them purpose and meaning? What kinds of choices did the inmates make that led them to chase the *right* things?

Why Is Choice Important? Questions for Teachers

CHOOSE

The single clenched fist lifted and ready,
Or the open asking hand held out and waiting.
Choose:
For we meet by one or the other.[3]

—Carl Sandburg

- How did Ma *meet* her students?

- How was she able to turn the clenched fists into open hands? How was she able to "turn thugs into poetry-reciting, thinking human beings"?

- How did Ma help the inmates make beneficial choices?

Notes

Preface

1. Josephson Institute of Ethics, "The Ethics of American Youth: Violence and Substance Abuse" [www.josephsoninstitute.org/Survey2000/violence2000-pressrelease.htm], Apr. 2, 2001.

2. National Institutes of Health, National Institute of Child Health and Human Development, "Bullying Widespread in U.S. Schools, Survey Finds" [www.nih.gov/news/pr/apr2001/nichd-24.htm], Apr. 2001.

3. Massachusetts Department of Public Health, "Suicide and Self-Inflicted Injury in Massachusetts 1996–1998" (Boston: Massachusetts Department of Public Health, May 9, 2001).

4. S. Covey, *Seven Habits of Highly Effective People* (West Valley City, Utah: Franklin Covey, 1990).

5. To learn more about these schools, see Character Education Partnership and Center for the Advancement of Ethics and Character at Boston University, *National Schools of Character 1998* (New York: McGraw-Hill, 1998); *National Schools of Character 1999* (Washington, D.C.: Character Education Partnership, 1999); and *National Schools of Character 2000* (Washington, D.C.: Character Education Partnership, 2000). To order these books or to obtain further information on the National Schools of Character Awards Program, please contact the Character Education Partnership, 1025 Connecticut Avenue NW, Suite 1011, Washington, D.C. 20036, (202) 296-7743, (800) 988-8081, fax: (202) 296-7779, Web site: www.character.org.

The schools selected as National Schools of Character in 1998 are Benjamin Franklin Classical Charter School, Franklin, Massachusetts; Brookside Elementary School, Binghamton, New York; Buck Lodge Middle School, Adelphi, Maryland; Easterling Primary School, Marion, South Carolina; Hazelwood Elementary School, Louisville, Kentucky; James E. McDade

Classical School, Chicago, Illinois; Mound Fort Middle School, Ogden, Utah; Mountain Pointe High School, Phoenix, Arizona; Newsome Park Elementary School, Newport News, Virginia; Pattonville High School, Maryland Heights, Missouri.

The 1999 Schools of Character are St. Leonard Elementary School, St. Leonard, Maryland; Atlantis Elementary School, Cocoa, Florida; Marion Intermediate School, Marion, South Carolina; Traut Core Knowledge School, Fort Collins, Colorado; Hilltop Elementary School, Lynnwood, Washington; Talent House Private School, Fairfax, Virginia; An Achievable Dream Academy, Newport News, Virginia; Kennedy Middle School, Eugene, Oregon; Montrose School, Natick, Massachusetts; Youth Opportunities Unlimited, San Diego, California; Wake County Public Schools, Raleigh, North Carolina.

The 2000 Schools of Character are Columbine Elementary School, Woodland Park, Colorado; Cotswold Elementary School, Charlotte, North Carolina; Emperor Elementary School, San Gabriel, California; Excelsior Academy, San Diego, California; Kennerly Elementary School, St. Louis, Missouri; Longfellow Elementary School, Hastings, Nebraska; Morgan Road Elementary School, Liverpool, New York; South Carroll High School, Sykesville, Maryland; Walnut Hill Elementary School, Dallas, Texas; Mt. Lebanon School District, Pittsburgh, Pennsylvania.

Chapter One

1. Aristotle, *The Nicomachean Ethics,* David Ross, trans. (New York: Oxford University Press, 1925).

2. Princeton Religious Research Center, *Emerging Trends,* Dec. 1993.

Chapter Two

1. P. S. Buck, *The Joy of Children* (New York: Day, 1964).

2. Aristotle, *The Nicomachean Ethics,* David Ross, trans. (New York: Oxford University Press, 1925), I.1.1103a34-7.

Chapter Four

1. L. Rosenblatt, *The Reader, the Text, the Poem* (Carbondale: Southern Illinois University Press, 1978), p. 44.

Chapter Six

1. Public Agenda Foundation, "Getting By: What American Teenagers Really Think About Their Schools" [www.publicagenda.org], Feb. 11, 1998.

2. Philip Tate, personal communication, Apr. 1998.

Chapter Seven

1. D. Isaacs, *Character Building: A Guide for Parents and Teachers* (Dublin: Four Courts Press, 1976).

Appendix N

1. Shel Silverstein, "Sarah Cynthia Sylvia Stout Would Not Take the Garbage Out," in *Where the Sidewalk Ends* (New York: HarperCollins, 1974), pp. 70–71.

Appendix O

1. Carl Sandburg, "Choose," in *Rainbows Are Made: Poems by Carl Sandburg, selected by Lee Bennett Hopkins* (Orlando, Fla.: Harcourt Brace, 1984).

Appendix P

1. F. Stockman, "Ex-Inmates Owe Success to 'Ma,'" *Boston Globe,* Mar. 9, 2001.

2. M. Albom, *Tuesdays with Morrie* (New York: Doubleday, 1997), p. 43.

3. Carl Sandburg, "Choose," in *Rainbows Are Made: Poems by Carl Sandburg, selected by Lee Bennett Hopkins* (Orlando, Fla.: Harcourt Brace, 1984).

The Authors

KAREN E. BOHLIN is executive director of the Center for the Advancement of Ethics and Character and assistant professor of education at Boston University. Her dual research interests are how students learn to internalize virtuous dispositions over time and how literature sheds light on the movement of the heart toward moral excellence. A former middle and high school English teacher, she has worked closely with schools and educational corporations and agencies, and has conducted numerous student educational programs both here and abroad. She is the coauthor of *Building Character in Schools* (with Kevin Ryan, 1999) and has published articles in the *Journal of the Association of Teacher Education, Education Week,* and elsewhere. She is a member of the National Schools of Character Blue Ribbon Panel and the Association of Teacher Educators (ATE) National Commission on Character Education. She holds a B.A. degree in English Literature and a B.S. degree in secondary education from Boston College and M.A. and Ed.D. degrees from Boston University.

KEVIN RYAN is founder and director emeritus of the Center for the Advancement of Ethics and Character at Boston University. A former high school English teacher, Ryan has taught on the faculties of Stanford University, the University of Chicago, Harvard University, Ohio State University, and the University of Lisbon. He has written and edited eighteen books, among them *Moral Education: It Comes with the Territory* (1976); *Reclaiming Our Schools: A Handbook for Teaching Character, Academics, and Discipline* (with Ed Wynne, 1992); and *Building Character in Schools* (with Karen Bohlin, 1999). He has received the University of Pennsylvania's National Educator of the Year Award, the Paideia Society's Award for Educational Excellence, and the Character Education Partnership's Sanford N. McDonnell Lifetime Achievement Award.

He received his M.A. degree in the teaching of English from Columbia University Teachers College and his Ph.D. degree from Stanford University.

DEBORAH FARMER holds a B.S. degree in elementary education and a B.A. degree in English literature from Boston University. She has taught the fourth and seventh grades and serves as an adjunct faculty member at Boston University, teaching student teachers. She is also a freelance writer for the Character Education Partnership's National Schools of Character (NSOC) Project, a consultant for schools and school districts seeking to integrate character education, and the lead author of *Stepping Stones* (1999, 2000, 2001), a workbook used in faculty in-service seminars. Currently, she is also an administrator at a K–8 school in Massachusetts.

Index

23; importance of choice for, 147; partnerships between parents and, 18; reflection by, 27–29, 71; sample survey of perceived school environment for, 123–125; seven competencies of character education, 68–70, 69e; six ways to promote good character by, 64–67; structured opportunities to reflect on progress, 27–28; taking time to listen, 77; useful core virtue definitions for, 22e; ways to inspire your students, 77–78; ways to involve the, 101
Tigner, S. S., 105
Traut Core Knowledge School (Fort Collins), 27, 41–42
Truth, S. (Isabella Baumfree), 42, 131–134
Tuesdays with Morrie (Albom), 26

U
Understanding: "Ain't I a Woman" (Sojourner Truth), 133–134; curriculum to inspire, 40; described, 13–14; Developing Yearlong Theme on, 140; Envisioning Diligence lesson on, 135–136; fostering core virtue, 21, 23–24; Great Depression lesson focus on, 129–130; internalizing virtue of, 96; need for school curriculum focus on, 15–16; strategic planning for, 25

V
Values: defining, 11; distinguished from virtues and views, 10–12
Views: defining, 10–11; distinguished from virtues and values, 10–12
Virtues: Aristotle's definition of, 5; cardinal and related, 4e; curriculum use of materials to internalize, 40–41; defining, 11–12; distinguished from views and values, 10–12; educating for, 64; helping students internalize, 12–17; instructional and schoolwide framework for internalizing, 96; offering explanations for, 65; wisdom, 3–4. *See also* Community of virtue; Core virtues
Virtus moralis (virtue), 11

W
Wald, G., 143
Walnut Hill Elementary (Dallas), 80–81
What Virtue Looks Like (K–B Guide), 107–108
White, J., 21
Wiggins, M. S., 27
The will of the people argument, 7
Winfrey, O., 11
Winning at Teaching Without Beating Your Kids (Coloroso), 73
Wisdom (or good judgment or prudence), 3, 4e, 96
Women's Rights Conference (1851), 132
Worksheets: Curriculum Development: Building on Existing Materials to Internalize Virtue, 40–41; Identifying Core Virtues, 19
The World We Created at Hamilton High (Grant), 30
Worlton, M., 131

Z
Zinn, H., 143